Successful Selection Interviewing

Other HRM books from Blackwell Business

The Equal Opportunities Handbook
Helen Collins

Total Quality and Human Resources
Barrie Dale and Cary Cooper

The Handbook of Human Resource Planning
Gordon McBeath

Developments in the Management of Human Resources
John Storey

Women's Career Development
Barbara White, Charles Cox and Cary Cooper

Human Resource Management in Action Series

Series editor: Brian Towers

Successful Training Practice
Alan Anderson

Managing Performance Appraisal Systems
Gordon Anderson

European Employee Relations
Jeff Bridgford and John Stirling

Practical Employment Law
Paul Lewis

The Successful Management of Redundancy
Paul Lewis

Managing the Team
Mick Marchington

The Japanization of British Industry
Nick Oliver and Barry Wilkinson

Strategy and the Human Resource
Ken Starkey and Alan McKinlay

Handbook of Human Resource Management
Edited by Brian Towers

Successful Selection Interviewing

Neil Anderson and Vivian Shackleton

First published 1993

Blackwell Publishers
108 Cowley Road
Oxford   OX4 1JF
UK

238 Main Street
Cambridge, Massachusetts 02142
USA

British Library Cataloguing in Publication Data
A CIP catalogue record for this book is available from the British Library.

Library of Congress Cataloging-in-Publication Data
Anderson, Neil (Neil D.)
     Successful selection interviewing / Neil Anderson and Vivian
Shackleton.
          p.   cm.
     Includes bibliographical references and index.
     1. Employment interviewing.   2. Employee selection.
I. Shackleton, V. J.   II. Title.
HF5549.5.I6A53   1993
658.3'1124 — dc20   92–40890
                                                              CIP

ISBN 0–631–188738

Typeset in 11 on 13 pt Plantin
by Graphicraft Typesetters Ltd, Hong Kong
Printed in Great Britain by T. J. Press, Padstow, Cornwall

Contents

List of Tables

List of Figures

List of Case Examples

Acknowledgements

Several colleagues and friends have helped us at various stages in the long haul to preparing this book. We would express our thanks to Yasmin Frings, Karen Gillespie, Phil Leather, Tim Payne and Bob Wareing for their constructive comments on earlier drafts of various chapters. Colleagues at the MRC/ESRC Social and Applied Unit, Sheffield University, provided the initial impetus for this project, especially Mike West and Nigel Nicholson, to whom the first author extends his sincere thanks for tolerating his 'skunk works' activities. To our wives, Elena and Margaret, we owe an invaluable debt of gratitude for their endless patience and moral support. Last, but by no means least, we must thank Katherine Hewitt, Charlotte Dewey, Sue Jeffery and Denise Curtis for their unstinting help over the months in transforming our illegible manuscripts into typographical works of art. Thank you all.

Neil Anderson
University of Nottingham

Viv Shackleton
Aston University

1
Inter-views of the Interview

Interviews in Practice: Popularity and Faith Validity

Selection interviews remain by far the most popular method of selecting candidates for jobs. They are ubiquitous. The interview is used regardless of the type of job being recruited for, its seniority in the organizational hierarchy, or the sector of industry involved, be it private or public sector, manufacturing, services, finance or whatever.

But why is the interview so overwhelmingly popular? To the recruiting organization it is an indisposable and objective assessment technique. In an interview the candidate is seen face-to-face, and so it is felt that an evaluation can be made of their personality, abilities, intelligence, and overall suitability for the job in question. Conversely, to the applicant the interview represents a major barrier to entry, a *rites de passage*, which has to be negotiated successfully in order to secure an offer of gainful employment. But it also provides a valuable opportunity to 'see the organization from the inside', to experience a fleeting glimpse of its culture, and to meet with its designated representative – the interviewer.

So, interviews are both *favoured* and *expected* as an indisposable part of the selection process by organizations and applicants alike. But there are other, equally compelling, reasons to explain why the interview remains popular. These include:

- *Interviewers strongly believe that they work* – that is, recruiters have faith in the validity of their own interviews to accurately select people for jobs.[1]
- *Interviews provide a forum for two-way information exchange* – the interview allows bilateral communication between the organization and the

candidate in a way that other selection techniques do not. It therefore provides precisely what its name suggests, an 'inter-view', with both parties meeting the other and forming an impression of them (Farr, 1982).

● *Interviews are a valued public relations exercise* – candidates take away vivid impressions of the organization and will undoubtedly share them with their friends and family.

● *Recruiters enjoy interviewing* – the role of the interviewer bestows an unusual amount of power on the recruiter, enabling them to probe into the personal details of a complete stranger – the interviewee.

● *Recruiters and candidates prefer to trust information 'seen with their own eyes'* – so even where other assessment techniques such as psychological tests are used, people tend to give most credence to their impressions gleaned from the interview (Herriot, 1987).

It appears then that the interview is here to stay, at least for the foreseeable future. The question is, how can we maximize its contribution to recruitment and selection procedures, and thus in the longer term, to match people to jobs, and jobs to people?

Aims and Objectives: Why Another 'How to Interview' Guide?

Our aims and objectives in writing this book stem directly, but only partly, from this continued and widespread use of interview for selection purposes. So, putting our heads on the block, what objectives did we have in mind when embarking upon *Successful Selection Interviewing*? It is true that over the years a hefty number of 'how to interview' guidebooks have built up on booksellers shelves, so why add another to the already bewildering choice facing the purchaser?

Our aims for this text are threefold.

1 *To provide a 'linking-text' which bridges the gulf between academic research into selection interviewing and informed practice by recruiters* – This is our pre-eminent objective. Despite eighty years of international research into interview processes, few of these academic study findings have been translated into practice by personnel practitioners. Instead potentially dangerous misconceptions abound, arguably fuelled by a number of not entirely accurate 'how to interview' guidebooks. Our intention here is to translate the mass of

research study findings into clear, practical advice for interviewers and interviewees, and so to offer an informed account of professional interview practices.

2 *To offer a text able to support professional skills training for students of Human Resource Management and Occupational Psychology* – The disciplines of Personnel Management/Human Resources Management (HRM) and Occupational Psychology have both become progressively more professional over the last two decades under the auspices of their respective professional associations, the Institute of Personnel Management and the British Psychological Society. Interview skills training now forms an integral part of the professional training syllabus for both the IPM and the BPS. We believe, therefore, that there is a demonstrable need for a comprehensive and up-to-date text on successful selection interviewing based upon research knowledge of interview processes and outcomes.

3 *To update selection practitioners on recent developments in interview theory, strategies and techniques* – On the assumption that the majority of practising recruiters are interested in developments in their field, our objective here is to provide an accessible account of the major advances in selection interviewing over recent years.

Particularly notable strides have been made in structured interview methods, for instance, which we cover in chapter 4. However, other developments are just as compelling, including:

• The use of biodata inventories, realistic job previews, psychometric tests, work samples, and assessment centres to complement the selection interview (see chapter 2).
• Candidate rating and assessment procedures using statistical and visual-perceptual algorithms to aid decision making (see chapter 7).
• Changes in employment law and equal opportunities legislation (see chapter 8).

It is therefore desirable to describe these developments as they relate to interview practices and to examine their impact upon the use of the interview in selection procedures.

Upon these three objectives should be superimposed our longer-term aim for this book – to help to improve interview practices in

ABC Holdings PLC wishes to appoint an assistant marketing manager on a starting salary of £14,000 per annum and expects a five-year length of service before the appointee is either promoted or leaves the organization. Profit sharing bonus is ten per cent of the salary per annum. Employer's National Insurance contributions are approximate at present-day values. Employer's pension contributions are calculated at fifteen per cent of salary per annum.

Employment costs	£
Salary: £14,000 x 5	70,000
Profit sharing bonus: £14,000 x 10% x 5	7,000
Employers N.I. Contributions (approx)	5,000
Employers pension contributions (approx)	10,500
	92,500

Selection costs	
Advertisement expenses	2,000
Selection expenses (interviewing, etc.)	2,000
Administration expenses (correspondence, etc.)	1,000
	5,000

Training costs	
Year 1 of job tenure	5,000
Year 2 of job tenure	4,000
Years 3,4, and 5 of job tenure	6,000
	15,000

Total	£112,500

Comments

This costing excludes salary increments over the period caused by inflation, employment overheads and relocation expenses. It also takes no account of the potential losses stemming from reduced efficiency if an ineffective job performer is recruited. Hence, the real costs will in point of fact be considerably greater.

Figure 1.1 Selection as an investment decision: the real costs.

industry. Interview practices have languished behind improvements in practice in other selection and assessment techniques (Smith and Robertson, 1986), and, almost certainly, every reader of this book would be able to recount personal experiences of being treated poorly by at least one selection interviewer.

Interviews as Investment Decisions

Because the interview is so commonplace and because many interviewers have inordinate confidence in their decision making abilities, there is a tendency to underestimate the skills needed to perform successful selection interviews. More importantly, because hundreds or perhaps even thousands of interviews are conducted every day of the working week few recruiters calculate in detail the actual costs involved in the selection process.

To illustrate this point, figure 1.1 analyses the costs of recruiting for a vacancy at a typical junior supervisor grade within an organization.

Even ignoring ongoing costs, such as salary increments, inflation, and unseen employment overheads, this selection process represents an investment decision of over £112,000. And we have purposely under-estimated the training costs involved with this type of skilled, supervisory position. Moreover, there are other hidden, much greater, potential costs incurred by recruiting the wrong person for this position. Recent research (Smith and Robertson, 1986) shows that, at a supervisory level, the difference between highly effective job incumbents and those who are less effective can be 40 per cent of salary per annum. So in this case we can add another £5,600 each year, or a total of £28,000 over the anticipated five-year tenure. But what about potentially costly mistakes and missed business opportunities in the worst-case scenario of appointing a particularly lackluster person to this job? Well, even at a conservative estimate, the costs will have topped the £250,000 barrier.

Yet, surprisingly, organizations are still quite prepared to select for such posts on the basis of a one-page application form followed by a 30-minute unstructured interview. Suggest to a technical director that they should make an investment decision to buy-in new equipment valued at a quarter of a million pounds on the basis of a one-page product specification and a half-hour conversation with a sales representative and they would rightly balk at the suggestion!

Yet this is precisely how many organizations continue to select for even senior positions.

The point is that while selection is undeniably a costly process, the potential losses incurred from making inaccurate appointments are disproportionately greater. But they are often hidden from view and only realized in the most extreme circumstances where the organization is forced to reappoint. So the importance of reaching accurate decisions 'first time around' cannot be overstated. And the interview, as the mainstay of many organizations' selection procedures, has a central role in this human resource investment decision process.

Structure of the Book

Successful Selection Interviewing is divided into three parts:

● Part I: Interviews in Context
● Part II: The Skills of Successful Selection Interviewing
● Part III: Interviews in Practice

Part I: Interviews in Context

The three chapters forming this part of the book serve to provide a context for the interview within wider organizational selection practices and the existing body of research into interviewer decision making.

In chapter 2 we consider recruitment and selection processes in detail, arguing that a *systems perspective* needs to be taken to the activities which comprise the selection process. By conceiving of the selection system as a series of inter-related and inter-dependent stages, we examine the 'fit' of the interview within the procedure. We also assess how interviews can be complimented by other methods of candidate assessment including psychometric tests of ability and personality, work samples, and multiple-method assessment centres. In fact, we conclude that there is no such thing as 'the interview', but three distinct types of interview being conducted at different stages in the selection process – the *mutual preview interview*, the *assessment interview*, and the *negotiation interview*.

Developing these themes, chapter 3 focuses specifically on the findings of over eight decades of empirical research by occupational psychologists into interview processes and interviewer decision making. Although the range of errors in interviewer decision making uncovered by research is undeniably worrying, we conclude that some beliefs (e.g., that interviewers reach outcome decisions in the first few minutes of the interview) remain far from vindicated. Indeed, recent research has shown the interview to be significantly more accurate than perhaps many thought to be the case, as long as it is structured and based upon detailed job analysis methodology.

Not surprisingly, the final chapter in part I, chapter 4, addresses the thorny issues of interview structure and format, posing the question: 'How structured should the interview be?'. We conclude that there is no one best way to structure all interviews, but that there are appropriate formats and degrees of structure for different types of interview.

Part II: The Skills of Successful Selection Interviewing

If part I of this book deals with the *context* surrounding successful selection interviews, part II deals specifically with *content issues*. Developing what we term a 'cognitive-social skills model' of interviewing, the three chapters comprising part II describe this model in practice. The model identifies two domains of related skills needed by the interviewer – *cognitive* skills of information processing and decision making, and *social* skills of managing the interaction process and eliciting information in an appropriate and professional manner.

In chapter 5 we describe the skills necessary to prepare for the interview, arguing that these steps are too often overlooked by recruiters. We subdivide these skills into five areas – location and set-up, general documentation, interview rating procedures, question generation and hypothesis formulation, and closing-down and following-up. In conclusion, we assert that interviewers need to be aware of, and practised in, these preparatory skills, and that such skills are of paramount importance for accurate decision making at interview.

The following chapter, chapter 6, considers in depth the social and interpersonal skills needed for successful selection interviews. As any interview is a two-way process, we describe skills from both the perspective of the interviewer and from that of the interviewee. Interviewers, we assert, need to posses and apply six types of social skill – rapport development, empathic listening, process management, questioning strategies, note-taking, and closing-down the interview. From the viewpoint of the interviewee, we define three types of skill – preparation, presentation, and persistency.

An interview has been described as a conversation with a purpose, the purpose being for both sides to reach a decision – for the interviewer whether to accept or reject the candidate, and for the candidate whether to accept any offer of employment. So, in chapter 7 we evaluate such decision making processes and strategies. In contrast with chapter 2, however, our concerns here are highly pragmatic ones. First, we examine the range of candidate assessment typologies available to the interviewer. Second, we describe decision making algorithms in practice. And third, we evaluate how recruiters can combine data from multiple selection methods and how they can allocate an appropriate weight to ratings of the candidate made at interview.

Part III: Interviews in Practice

Part III continues the practical theme by looking at two crucial topics for interviews – staying within the spirit and the letter of the law, and the training of the interviewers.

Chapter 8 is concerned with two acts which impinge directly on the conduct of the employment interview, the Sex Discrimination Acts of 1975 (and 1986) and the 1976 Race Relations Act. To comply with these acts all selection procedures, including the screening of candidates, questions asked in the interview, who is offered employment and the employment terms offered that person, must be fair, irrespective of sex, race or ethnic group. We look at examples of fair and unfair practices and examine cases which have been brought before industrial tribunals claiming sex or race discrimination.

Chapter 9 concludes both this section and the book by examining practical ways of improving interviewer skills through training. It takes the reader through analysis of training needs and the principles of effective training to the design of a programme and an evaluation of its effectiveness. Along the way we consider whether the training should be conducted by tutors from other organizations (open courses) or tailor-made for the particular organization. We also discuss and compare the main training methods, including lectures, discussions, videos, films, role play exercises and 'real-life' interviews. Finally, we emphasize that CCTV (closed circuit television) and constructive feedback play a crucial role if participants are to get the most from an interviewer training programme.

Summary Propositions

1 Interviews remain an overwhelmingly popular method of selecting candidates for jobs. This is because:
   (a) Interviewers believe that interviews are effective;
   (b) They provide a forum for two-way information exchange;
   (c) They are a valued public relations exercise;
   (d) Recruiters enjoy interviewing; and
   (e) Recruiters and candidates prefer to trust information 'seen with their own eyes.'
2 In this book we aim to:
   (a) Provide a text which links academic research and selection interviewing practices;
   (b) Offer support for interviewer training;
   (c) Update HRM practitioners on recent developments in interview theory, strategies and techniques.
3 Selection interviewing involves making decisions which constitute substantial investments in human resources for the organization.

Notes

1   See also Anderson, N. R. (1993) Eight decades of interview research: A retrospective metareview and prospective commentary, *The European Work and Organizational Psychologist*, 2, 1–32.

References

Farr, R. (1982) Interviewing: the social psychology of the interview, in *Psychology and People*, A. J. Chapman and A. Gale (eds) London: BPS/Macmillan).
Herriot, P. (1987) The selection interview, in Psychology at Work, P. Warr (ed.) (Harmondsworth: Penguin).
Smith, M. and Robertson I. T. (1986) *The Theory and Practice of Systematic Staff Selection*, (London: Macmillan).

Part I
Interviews in Context

The three chapters forming this part of the book provide a context for successful selection interviewing. It is only through gaining an appreciation of this context of selection systems in practice that the interview may be designed and conducted in a way that contributes significantly to staff resourcing decisions and thus to Human Resource Management strategies and practices. The interview, once conceptualized within this systemic framework, is an invaluable tool for information sharing, assessment, and negotiation between the organization and the applicant.

2
Systems of Selection and the Role of the Interview

'Good selection interviewing depends mostly on the efficient use of a system for selection in which the interview itself plays only a small part'

McHenry, *The Selection Interview*, 1981

Systems of Selection: Signing-On

Our aim in this chapter is to 'place the interview in context'. That is, to examine the role of the interview in relation to other selection techniques commonly conducted as part of an organization's selection procedure. We aim to answer four key questions:

1 What can the interview contribute to personnel selection procedures?
2 Where does the interview 'fit' in the overall scheme of organizational selection procedures?
3 What other methods commonly supplement the interview in selection systems?
4 What advice can be offered for maximizing the contribution of the interview to accurate selection decisions?

Case example 2.1 probably sounds all too familiar to many personnel and line managers responsible for recruiting staff into their organizations. Indeed, it is based upon actual circumstances from the authors' own experiences as recruiters in industry. 'It should never have happened', is the response that springs immediately to mind. But, just how often must this expression be heard in personnel departments all over the country?

This case example raises a number of questions to do with the planning and design of recruitment procedures. For instance, why did this situation arise in the first place? How can HRM specialists deal with such high response rates? What should be done to deal with interference and personal bias by management colleagues? And, of course, what can be done to avoid such situations occurring in the future?

It is to answer these and similar questions that this chapter is devoted. It also provides a foundation for the following chapters of the book. Here we consider the overall process of recruitment and selection, the relation between different stages in this process, and the interconnections between the selection interview and other assessment techniques. The 'fit' of the interview within the procedure is carefully appraised and recommendations for the design of effective systems for selection are put forward in conclusion.

Case Example 2.1

The real-life pressures of selection

David Burrows, personnel officer for a multinational insurance company, ponders his current predicament. After placing a display advertisement in a local evening newspaper for an accounts clerk in the company's financial services department his desk is now swamped with over 200 handwritten applications of all shapes and sizes, all awaiting his personal attention. His telephone is constantly occupied by applicants enquiring about the success or otherwise of their own CV. More importantly, at least as far as David Burrows is concerned, a less than flattering internal telephone call from the finance director this morning has much annoyed him. Apparently both the finance director's son and niece applied over three weeks ago, but 'have heard nothing whatsoever since'. David Burrows, feeling unusually under stress and embattled, settles back in his chair and resigns himself to the task of sifting through each and every application in turn.

Questions

1 How should David Burrows decide who to reject?
2 Should he bow to pressures of organizational politics and interview the finance director's relatives regardless of their merits as applicants?
3 After reading this chapter, how could a systems approach to this selection procedure assist David Burrows?

The Systems Approach to Recruitment and Selection

Although still the most popular method for assessing applicants, the interview cannot stand alone as the be-all-and-end-all of organizational selection procedures. The interview should be treated as only one stage in a multi-stage process. It stands in relation to, and is influenced by, the other methods and procedures comprising the overall procedure. This approach, best termed a *systems approach to selection* is based on three fundamental assumptions:

- That any recruitment and selection system is comprised of a series of *inter-related* and *inter-connected* stages;
- That later stages are *chronologically dependent* upon preceding stages in the system;
- That each stage of assessment is both a *predictor* and an *affector* of the candidates future behaviour.

Let us consider briefly each of these in turn.

1 *Inter-related components: 'Common sense is not necessarily common practice'* – It is undeniably common sense to view the overall selection system as a series of inter-related and inter-connected stages. Unfortunately, as the saying goes, 'common sense is not necessarily common practice'. The wording of any job advertisement will clearly affect the range of applications received; the design of the application form will govern the information provided by candidates and influence interviewer questioning strategies; the results of psychological tests may impinge upon details requested in any subsequent letter of reference, and so forth. The point is that the 'output' from earlier selection methods (i.e., the pool of applicants remaining within the procedure) forms the 'input' for later methods in the selection system. Later stages are thus *chronologically dependent* upon all earlier stages.

2 *Chronological dependency* – Selection systems exist to discriminate between applicants who are likely to be successful job performers in the future and those who are not. The design of selection systems has three objectives:

- To discriminate or 'predict' job performance with some accuracy and consistency;
- To discriminate between applicants on grounds which are both lawful and ethical; and

● To maximize predictive accuracy in relation to the costs of operating the selection system.

In our experience, organizations all too often overlook chronological dependency in their systems of recruitment. For example, many run expensive and sophisticated multi-day, multi-method 'assessment centres', but at the same time pre-screening applicants through a cursory review of their application details. Another example is where comprehensive and detailed job analysis has been omitted and only hazy and partially correct criteria are used to select for initial interview. We consider the implications of chronological dependency later in this chapter, but it is certainly the case that later stages of selection can only ever be as accurate as the decisions made in earlier stages to pre-screen down numbers of candidates remaining in the procedure.

3 *Predictors and affectors* – The third assumption underlying the systems approach to recruitment concerns our view that assessment techniques are both *predictors* and *affectors* of the future behaviour of the applicant in the job. Interviewers often conveniently overlook this two-way relationship, treating candidates poorly and even abusively at times. The implication is that interviewees treated in this way may not accept any resulting offer of employment, and even if they do, they may well be less motivated to perform the job to their true ability. This *affective component* of selection systems remains especially true, of course, for the best candidates who are probably just as attractive to competitor employers. Organizations can therefore inadvertently reduce the absolute level of predictive accuracy of their selection systems by disregarding the affective component of their system by treating candidates in ways which persuade them either to withdraw or to perform the job less well. By treating candidates in a slipshod manner, the best may never accept offers of employment, thus reducing the top-end of the range of performers who actually join the organization. Placing a *false ceiling* of maximal performance in this way clearly reduces the effectiveness of an organization's selection procedure.

Selection Systems: Common Configurations

Having outlined these three principal assumptions of the systems approach, we can proceed to examine how selection systems operate in practice, and to examine the role of interviews in the procedure. We should note at this early stage that often the interview serves as the sole method of assessment in the procedure, perhaps supplemented only by a cursory reference from previous employers. As this is the case, we focus quite specifically in this chapter on the majority of organizations who may be considering supplementing the interview with other more sophisticated methods of candidate assessment. Figure 2.1 illustrates perhaps the most common configuration, with the system comprising four stages:

1 Recruitment
2 Pre-screening
3 Candidate assessment
4 Induction

Phase I: Recruitment

1 *Recognition of the need for new human resources* – Stimuli for recognizing the need for new personnel come in two forms – short-term reactive and long-term strategic. Of the first type, the level of staff turnover within the organization is of major concern. This outflow of personnel, however, should merely signal the need to consider replacements only after a detailed review of work methods and task allocation has been conducted within the section affected. All too often one encounters the *automatic replacement syndrome* whereby vacancies created by staff leaving are immediately filled without a proper review of work organization being undertaken to reveal potential improvements in working practices among the remaining personnel[1]. As highlighted in chapter 1, recruitment is a costly business and organizations would be well-advised to consider options created by the redistribution or reorganization of workload initially, resorting to selection only if absolutely necessary. Longer term stimuli for recruitment stem from the organization's business and strategic plans – for example, where the organization plans to expand or diversify into new product areas demanding skills and abilities not within the organization at present. Again, recruitment should not be seen as a panacea cure, but as only one of a range of options to meet such longer term objectives.

2 *Job Analysis* – Job analysis has been defined by the Department of Employment as '. . . the process of examining a job in order

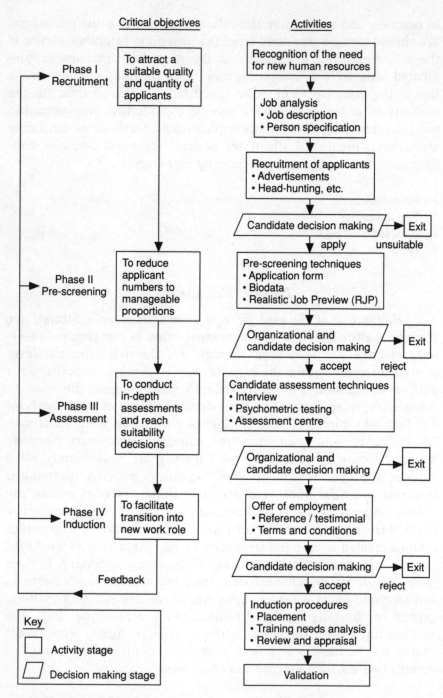

Figure 2.1   A systems model of recruitment and selection.

to identify its component tasks. The detail and approach may vary according to the purpose of which the job is being analysed' (1971). To do justice to the topic of job analysis requires a whole book covering the diversity of approaches and methods developed over many years by occupational psychologists (see Appendix II for recommended further reading). Here, we can only hope to present a concise summary of these techniques and to advise the reader to follow-up at least one of the specialized texts in this area. So, what exactly is job analysis and why is it seen as the foundation of the systems approach to selection? Job analysis subdivides into two related processes, the *job description*, and the *person specification*.

Job analysis involves breaking down a job into its component parts to produce a written job description moving from more general activities to highly specific task elements. This produces a hierarchical listing of component tasks, as follows. The job of training officer is broken down firstly into job activities, secondly into task components, and thirdly into task elements. To illustrate this hierarchical breakdown, the first task activity, 'to design and conduct training programmes', subdivides into three task components – course presentation, preparation of training materials, and evaluation and feedback. The task component of course presentation further subdivides into four task elements, and so forth. The job description could be broken down as follows:

1 Job title – Training officer
2 Job activities – To design and conduct training programmes
3 Task components –
   (a) course presentation
   (b) preparation of training materials
   (c) evaluation and feedback
4 Task elements –
   (a) reviewing literature
   (b) summarizing literature
   (c) developing course itineraries
   (d) developing training plans

Job analysis methods vary considerably in the depth of detail entered into, ranging from broad descriptions of general job contents to detailed reports and timings of operator movements and muscular actions. Four main methods of data collection are commonly used:

- *Interviewing* the job incumbent, their peers, their immediate supervisor, etc. Interviewing is still the most popular method of data collection.
- *Observing* the job while it is being performed. This requires the skills of a professionally trained job analyst using a validated system of observation.
- *Questionnaires* completed by the job incumbent, peers, or supervisor.
- *Documented records* relating to job tasks, methods, and objectives.

However detailed the job analysis procedure, and whichever method is used, the objective remains basically the same – to provide a framework in the form of the job description to drive the recruitment and selection process[2].

The job description forms the basis of the second part of the job analysis process – the person specification. Whereas the job description lays down the tasks comprising the job, the person specification sets out the skills and abilities needed to perform these tasks. Again, as with job descriptions, a whole range of person specifications are to be found in use in personnel selection, but most cover aspects of the candidates educational qualifications, professional training, personality, and key skills needed to perform the job under scrutiny (Rodger, 1952; Fraser, 1978). In effect, the person specification translates the job specification into the skills and abilities needed to perform job tasks.

Together, the job description and person specification form the bedrock of the selection processes as they establish the *criteria* against which applications will be screened. These will vary depending upon the type of vacancy involved. Nonetheless, the importance of generating an accurate job description and person specification cannot be understated.

Case example 2.2 illustrates the pitfalls of slacking on this process. Two companies, each receiving 200 applicants each year for 30 clerical vacancies, differ in the accuracy of their screening criteria and method of job analysis. Company A uses up-to-date and detailed job descriptions and person specifications to generate relevant and appropriate criteria for pre-screening applicants. Company B, on the other hand, relies on 'gut feeling' and rather outdated and incomplete descriptions and specifications. The results – Company A achieves eighty per cent decision making accuracy at this stage, Company B only fifty per cent. This in itself is a cause for concern, but further statistics reveal that Company A has incorrectly retained only twenty unsuitable applicants going on to final interview, whereas this proportion is 50 out of 100 in Company B. Clearly, the chances of reaching accurate selection decisions for the 30 vacancies are substantially better in Company A than in Company B, regardless of their method of final decision making.

This case example illustrates the importance of getting the early stages of a selection system right. In terms of chronological dependency, we again emphasize the need for organizations to conduct detailed job analysis as the foundation stone of their selection systems.

Case Example 2.2

The 'chronological dependency' of personnel selection systems

	Company A	Company B
Number of clerical applications per annum	200	200
Number of vacancies	30	30
State of job descriptions and person specifications	Good – updated regularly to ensure accuracy. Also quite complete and detailed	Poor – incomplete record based upon out-of-date job analysis procedures
Screening criteria	Specific and clearly stated – screening decisions always made on the basis of these formal criteria	Unclear and unspecified screening decisions made on the basis of 'gut feeling'
Number of applicants rejected on the basis of application form details	100	100
Number of applications incorrectly rejected – those who could have	20	50

performed the job satisfactorily ('false negatives')		
Number of applications retained incorrectly, i.e. those who could not perform the job satisfactorily ('false positives')	20	50
Percentage of 'false positives' remaining in the applicant pool	10%	25%
Proportion of unsuitable applications incorrectly retained and going forward to later phases	1 in 10 (total = 20)	1 in 4 (total = 50)
Proportion of suitable candidates incorrectly rejected from the system	1 in 10 or 10% (total = 20)	1 in 4 or 25% (total = 50)
Decision making accuracy Number of correct decisions/total number of decisions	$\frac{160}{200} = 80\%$	$\frac{100}{200} = 50\%$

3   *Recruitment of applicants* – Once the job analysis procedure has been completed the next stage is to attract a suitable quantity of applicants with the desired qualities. A range of methods can be used, including:

- Internal advertisement
- Eliciting applications from relatives and friends of employers
- External advertisement
- Job Centres
- Recruitment agencies
- Executive search organizations

The choice of method will depend upon the vacancy to be filled, time constraints, cost limitations, and existing custom and practice within the organization. The possibility of discriminating indirectly against certain groups will also limit the use of methods such as word of mouth (see chapter 8). Seasoned recruiters are well aware of one of the tensions at this stage in the selection process – the *attraction-rejection dilemma*. That is, early on recruiters have a responsibility to attract candidates to apply, whom, as time goes on, they know they may well have to reject as less suitable. Of course, accurate job descriptions and person specifications help to minimize this dilemma by giving the recruiter the confidence that decisions are being reached based upon appropriate and fair criteria.

Phase II: Pre-screening

All pre-screening techniques share two common aims – to reduce the numbers of applicants to manageable levels for more detailed methods of assessment to be applied; and to reject unsuitable applicants while retaining the most suitable ones.

There are four possible methods for pre-screening:

- application forms
- biodata
- Realistic Job Previews (RJPs)
- other 'fringe' methods

1 Application forms Appearing in all shapes and sizes, the application form looks set to remain one of the most popular methods of initial information collection on candidates (Anderson and Shackleton, 1986). It structures data collection and thus possesses advantages over the non-uniformity of candidate CVs. However, organizations can lose sight of the purpose of the application form which is simply to facilitate pre-screening techniques based upon appropriate and relevant criteria.

Cast your thoughts back to David Burrows, our beleaguered personnel officer in case example 2.1 described at the beginning of this chapter. Faced with considerable pressures to reach pre-screening decisions quickly, he is reliant upon the design of each applicant's CV to highlight key criteria so as to assist him to recognize appropriate data in order to give them suitable weight in his decision making task.

Recent developments in occupation and cognitive psychology (Anderson and Shackleton, 1986) show that recruiters are often placed under information overload. By this it is meant that they are loaded with too much data to be able to cope. One likely response is that they 'satisfy' by simplifying the criteria used to reach decisions, for instance, by stereotyping candidates upon the basis of a couple of pieces of data (Anderson, 1992). We discuss these dangers in greater depth in chapters 3 and 4, but as far as application form design is concerned, the point to note is that important data should be easily recognizable and that the form should help rather than hinder the recruiter's cognitive processes of information recognition and processing. Not surprisingly, recent research has begun to examine these cognitive processes and the ways in which application forms need to be designed to maximize their usefulness to the recruiter (Anderson and Shackleton, 1986).

2 Biodata inventories Biodata (short for biographical data) inventories began to be seriously considered by recruiters in this country in the 1970s and 1980s. Comprising multiple biographical, behavioural, and attitudinal questions (or so-called 'items'), the design of a biodata inventory is based on statistical correlation with subsequent job performance. As biodata inventories can require a relatively large pool of recruits to permit the calculation of such statistics, they have tended to be used at lower levels of an organizational hierarchy where larger numbers of recruits are taken on each year (e.g., graduate and clerical selection).

Since these statistical procedures can become quite complex, we shall not dwell upon biodata instruments here, save to point out that it is advisable for organizations considering the use of biodata inventories to take advice from a chartered occupational psychologist registered under the auspices of the relevant professional association, the British Psychological Society.

3 Realistic Job Previews (RJPs) RJPs, in terms of their chronological position in a selection system, can come before even the application form, CV, or biodata inventory. As the term suggests, an RJP involves providing potential candidates with a realistic preview of the job vacancy in sufficient detail for an applicant to self-select in or out of the process. The initial advertisement is one method through which to do this and its wording should be given careful consideration. For instance, question:

• What requirements are called for in terms of qualifications, abilities, and special aptitudes?

- What type of personality is best suited to this vacancy?
- Are any special circumstances relevant – such as considerable travel away from home, clean driving licence, etc?

RJPs, if properly constructed, have been found to be an accurate and reliable method of pre-screening candidates (Anderson and Shackleton, 1986). Moreover, they are highly cost-effective as they rely upon the candidate to reach a decision concerning their own suitability for the job role in question before any candidate assessment method needs to be applied. Of course, the interview itself provides a further opportunity to utilize the RJP approach,[3] and we will consider this possibility in the following sections of this chapter.

4 'Fringe' methods 'Fringe' forms of pre-screening, including graphology (the interpretation of candidate handwriting to infer personality and ability), astrology (use of star signs), and even phrenology (the analysis of cranial physiognomy, or bumps on the head!), have all been reported as alternative methods to reduce candidate numbers to manageable proportions early in the selection procedure (Anderson and Shackleton, 1986). Unfortunately, the best that can be said of these fringe methods is that they are unproven in terms of their efficiency for pre-screening purposes. Given the importance of these early screening decisions, our advice is to stick to the well-validated and more mainstream techniques of application forms, biodata inventories, and RJPs.

It is important at this point to acknowledge that there now exist definitive expectations of professional conduct in dealing with applications received in any selection process. The Institute of Personnel Management lays down minimum standards of professional practice in its 1991 publication *The IPM Recruitment Code* (1991). These include:

Receipt of anticipated applications must be acknowledged by the recruiter. Unsolicited applications should be acknowledged wherever possible and given appropriate consideration. Prompt acknowledgment of applications is an example of good practice and good public relations, and will avoid vexatious claims under the Employment Act 1990.

Applications must be treated as confidential. The circulation of papers must be restricted to those involved in the recruitment and

selection process. Applications must not be passed on to other organizations without first obtaining the applicant's approval.

Where the recruiter uses the application form for pre-selection or screening, the information contained must only be judged against the job specification and person specification.

These are important and wholly laudable expectations of professional practice and it is worthwhile to emphasize that the IPM clearly perceives these as *minimum* standards for its members.

Phase III: Candidate Assessment

Once the number of candidates remaining within the procedure has been scaled down to manageable proportions, the business of in-depth assessment can begin. An extensive range of assessment methods is currently available to the recruiter. Our purpose here is to review briefly the major methods in common use today and, as we stated earlier, to give consideration to how each method can supplement the interview as the mainstay of most organizations' selection procedures. We have intentionally restricted the number of techniques reviewed in this chapter to the three most popular alternative or complementary methods to the interview:

- psychometric tests
- work samples
- assessment centres (ACs)

Table 2.1 summarizes these techniques and indicates their likely contribution to the overall selection system. Figure 2.2 illustrates the accuracy and the popularity of these methods on the basis of current research findings. Figure 2.2 reveals some intriguing findings. Firstly, it is not necessarily the most accurate methods which are the most popular. For instance, references are used by almost all organizations surveyed (Shackleton and Newell, 1991), but fall well down the 'league table' of predictive accuracy. Secondly, and perhaps a little surprisingly to some, the structured interview is a comparatively accurate assessment method. In fact, it betters all other techniques apart from assessment centres for promotion. Thirdly, the interview is universal – 100 per cent of organizations surveyed reported using it at one time or another. So, let us consider

Table 2.1 Main techniques of candidate assessment

Technique	Description	'Fit' with the interview	Contribution to the selection system
Psychometric testing	Standardized test of performance, attitudes, or personality. Major types • cognitive ability • personality • attitudes and values • career choice and guidance	Can precede or succeed the interview stage. Results can form the basis of further interview questions, or the interview can be used to feedback test results. Personality tests are particularly useful in this respect and can facilitate probing questions at interview.	*Ability tests* • High predictive accuracy for aspects of cognitive ability, see figure 2.2 • 'Normed' results allow testee to be compared with many other similar individuals • Longer-term relevance i.e., the job role may change over time; ability remains relatively constant *Personality tests* • Indications of interpersonal/ managerial style which can be followed up at interview and/or compared with performance in exercises in an AC • 'Faking' scales built into tests may detect high levels of impression management and biasing of self-presentation

Table 2.1 (*cont.*)

Technique	Description	'Fit' with the interview	Contribution to the selection system
Work samples	Pre-designed and constructed samples of work performance designed to tap aspects of critical job performance usually monitored and observed by trained experts who rate candidates on job-relevant dimensions.	Usually following initial interview and often conducted as part of an AC. Can therefore provide dynamic and highly job-relevant data for discussion at the follow-up interview stage.	• High predictive accuracy • Directly relevant job tasks as samples of future behaviour • Rated by observers on critical dimensions of job performance, sometimes identical to those used for staff appraisal • If constructed properly can add a sample of directly relevant candidate behaviour on segments of the job itself

Method	Description	Notes
Assessment Centres (ACs)	Multiple-method design usually incorporating testing, interviews, and work sample exercises, where candidates are rated by observers on job-relevant dimensions. Can last between one and five days.	Usually the final stage of assessment to reach outcome decisions due to the costs of running ACs. Interviews usually conducted as an integral part of an AC.	• All of the above, plus • An opportunity to observe candidates over a longer period of time in formal and informal situations • Multiple assessments by several assessors over several exercises can eliminate some individual biases associated with one-to-one interviews (see chapter 3)
Reference letter	Varies from being a very brief factual check (e.g., 'did the candidate hold this position between these dates as claimed?') to an extensive rating of abilities, personality and attitudes to work.	Commonly utilized as the final check upon the candidate after a conditional offer of employment has been made. The interview can throw up specific issues to be checked with previous employers by reference letter.	• Best utilized as a factual check only • Most appropriate as final check – references taken up with existing employers prior to an offer of employment will not be popular among candidates!

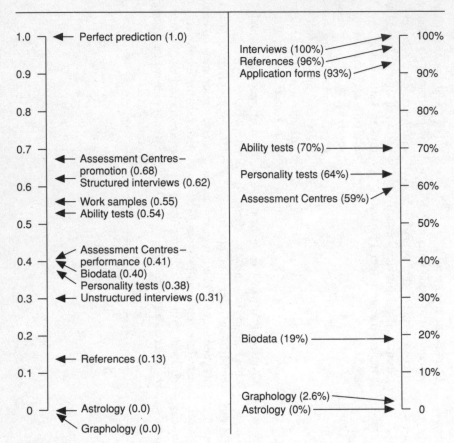

Figure 2.2 The predictive accuracy and popularity of assessment and pre-screening methods.

Notes

1   Predictive accuracy figures use a correlation scale, ranging from 0-chance prediction, to 1.0 – perfect prediction. Results based upon work by Mike Smith, University of Manchester, published in *Personnel Management* (December 1986) and updated to include recent reviews of the interview.

2   Popularity figures derived from Shackleton and Newell, *Journal of Occupational Psychology* (1991). Sample is of 73 British organizations. Percentages relate to methods used at some time during selection procedures.

each of these techniques in relation to their accuracy, their potential contribution to the selection system, and their fit with the selection interview.

Psychometric testing

Literally hundreds of tests are now on the market, all competing for the patronage (and finances!) of recruiting organizations. The two broad types of test most commonly used are tests of cognitive ability and tests of personality (Toplis, Dulewitz and Fletcher, 1987).

1 *Tests of cognitive ability* – As figure 2.2 shows, tests of cognitive ability rank quite highly on the league table of predictive accuracy, being bettered only marginally by ACs for promotion, structured interviews, and work sample tests. This is not the place for us to embark upon a detailed theoretical or statistical review of ability tests, since other more specialized texts on psychometric testing offer this already (Annastasi, 1988), we should, however, note the major types of ability test. These are tests of:

● General intelligence or 'IQ' – including various IQ tests and tests of general intelligence not intended for use in selection scenarios
● Numerical reasoning ability
  – specific ability to work with numerical data, or to examine relations between numbers and series of numbers (e.g., 3, 5, 8, 12, X?)
● Verbal reasoning ability
  – specific ability to interpret meaning correctly from passages of written text, or to establish the relationship between words (Hot is to Cold as Distant is to X?)
● Spatial and diagrammatic reasoning ability – establishing relationships between shapes or series of shapes
● Cognitive functioning ability
  – including tests of clerical speed and accuracy, filing accuracy, etc.

2 *Tests of personality* – As with tests of cognitive ability, the recruiter is currently spoilt for choice in terms of the sheer number of personality tests available to them. Table 2.2 identifies some of the most popular personality tests, but is certainly not intended as a definitive list. Some of these have been developed specifically for use in occupational assessment and selection (e.g., Saville and Holdsworth's Occupational Personality Test, or OPQ), while others have undergone extensive trials and revision to be used for selection

Table 2.2   Popular tests of cognitive ability and personality

Ability	*Personality*
GMA Graduate and Managerial Assessment Battery [ASE]	*16PF* The 16-Personality Factor Questionnaire (ASE)
VA1, VA3, NA2, NA4 Verbal and Numerical Series (Saville and Holdsworth)	*OPQ* The Occupational Personality Questionnaire (Saville and Holdsworth)
Ravens Progressive Matrices Ravens Progressive Matrices & Vocabulary Scale (NFER-Nelson)	*MBTI* Myers Briggs Type Indicator (Test Agency)
Watson-Glaser Watson-Glaser Test of Critical Thinking (Psychological Corp)	*CPI* California Personality Inventory (Oxford Psychologists Press)
TMA Thurstone Test of Mental Alertness (SRA/London House)	*EPI* Eysenck Personality Inventory (NFER-Nelson)

Notes
1 Test Supplies indicated within parentheses.
2 A list of the contact addresses of the major test suppliers is given in Appendix I toward the end of the book.

purposes in this country (e.g., the Anglicised version of 16PF test supplied by ASE Ltd).

Recruiters considering using personality tests as part of their assessment procedure need to consider the time taken to administer and score the test, requirements for training imposed by the test publishers, its validity and reliability as indicated in the test's statistical manual, as well as ensuring that the test is not discriminatory against one sex or employees from ethnic minorities.

Recent years have witnessed a considerable increase in the use of both ability and personality tests for selection in the UK (Shackleton and Newell, 1991). Table 2.2 summarizes the most popular tests at present, but it should be noted that not all tests are as respectable as those mentioned in this figure. Indeed, the recruiter needs to be wary of a small minority of less scrupulous test suppliers, particularly in the area of personality testing, where the rapid growth in this market has spawned a number of 'quick and dirty' tests of personality.

Whether buying-in tests of personality or ability it is advisable to:

- Ask the background of the test suppliers – are they chartered occupational psychologists, or not?
- Request an inspection copy of the manual accompanying the test – does it quote sufficient statistical evidence that the test is valid and reliable?
- Check out training requirements – respectable tests usually require test administration training and certification before users are allowed to buy the test.
- Be wary of 'quick fix' tests promising to solve all your selection difficulties at the drop-of-a-hat; do not take the 'it seems to assess me ok' test as the only indicator of value.
- Seek the advice of a professional test expert – the British Psychological Society, based in Leicester, keeps a register of qualified and experienced psychometricians.

Tests of ability and personality, if used properly, can contribute substantially to the accuracy and fairness of selection systems. Moreover, they often constitute the first method of assessment considered by organizations as complimentary to the selection interview. Thus, organizations wishing to improve the objectivity of their existing selection procedures based solely upon the interview often consider psychometric testing as the first step along this path. And quite rightly so. Tests are relatively cost-effective, potentially highly accurate and, perhaps more cynically, offer a novel area of esoteric expertise for personnel practitioners to gain credance in other departments of their organization!

But what can tests contribute which the interview cannot, and how can the two methods best be used in conjunction? The first point is that many organizations currently misuse the interview as a kind of quasi-ability and quasi-personality test. That is, they use the interview as an opportunity to gain a sample of behaviour from the candidate from which the interviewer infers or attributes ability and personality. We discuss in chapter 3 why this strategy is fraught with pitfalls. Suffice it to say here that the advantages of using proven tests of ability and personality overcome many of these difficulties and free-up the interview to perform other functions in the selection system, which we discuss later in this chapter.

The second point is that test results can be used in the interview if the tests are taken in advance. Here, for instance, the reasons for performance results on verbal or numerical tests can be investigated; the candidate's profile resulting from a personality test discussed with them; and last, but not least, the accuracy of test results can be validated against the applicant's self-perceptions and any incongruences probed.

To summarize, properly constructed tests of ability and personality work well. At a minimum they complement the selection interview and, if integrated fully into an organization's selection system, they can bolster the accuracy of the interview by generating unforeseen question areas for the interviewer to delve into. At best they can substantially improve the accuracy of selection decisions and also create a highly positive impression of the organization as far as candidates are concerned.

Work samples

Despite their predictive accuracy, comparatively few organizations use work samples (Anderson and Shackleton, 1986; Shackleton and Newell, 1991). As table 2.1 and figure 2.2 show, work samples can provide a valuable and dynamic sample of candidate behaviour on job-relevant dimensions. Perhaps it is because work samples require tailoring carefully to each job being recruited for that they are less popular than psychometric tests. Whatever the reasons for this undeserved lack of popularity, work samples again provide the opportunity to partial-out an area of predicting candidate behaviour which the interview presently attempts to cope with.

Imagine, for example, the common situation of an interviewer using the behaviour of the candidate during the interview to suppose that this is how they behave habitually and therefore to extrapolate that this is how the candidate will behave on the job. In fact, much of the research into interviewer decision making indicates that this is precisely what interviewers do (see chapter 3). Unfortunately, of course, the interview is a rather unusual social situation and, in the view of many candidates, some interviews appear to be particularly bizarre ones!

Using candidate behaviour at interview to predict job behaviour can be like using performance on a motorway services arcade car-racing machine to predict subsequent safety on a journey by car. To the extent that the two are alike (some motorways are indeed accurately modelled by video car-racing games!) it is sensible in theory to extrapolate interview behaviour to on-the-job behaviour. Usually, though, improvements in predictive accuracy accrue from separating out the two and using properly constructed work samples to perform this task.

Assessment centres (ACs)

Clive Fletcher, Professor of Occupational Psychology at the University of London defines an AC as 'assessment of a group of individuals by a team of judges using a comprehensive and integrated series of techniques' (Fletcher, 1982). Note that the term refers to the portfolio of techniques comprising an AC and the use of multiple judges as assessors rather than to a physical location or 'centre'. Since an AC usually takes several days to complete, the depth of assessment provided is unique. It is also more costly than administering tests or work samples alone, but many ACs incorporate tests, work samples and interviews within their design. Hence, the synergy between these component parts of an AC is crucial to overall predictive accuracy.

Much research attention has been devoted to investigating the most accurate way to combine ratings by several assessors on multiple dimensions across multiple exercises into the final Overall Assessment Rating (or OAR) given to each candidate. One danger revealed in a recent study into an AC used to select personnel for the British civil service is that the interview carried too much weight and influenced the OAR too extensively (Feltham, 1988). Combining ratings by use of a statistical model or algorithm can avoid this pitfall (see chapter 7). Another potential danger is the reluctance shown by many organizations to check that their AC actually works – that is, that it predicts future job success with acceptable accuracy and consistency. Their reasoning appears to be analogous to the tale of the emporer's new clothes. Recruiters sometimes reason that as their AC was designed by prestigious (and expensive) management consultants as state-of-the-art technology, that it costs considerable time and effort to operate, and in any case, that their line managers act as assessors and have not complained so far that they have selected inappropriate candidates into their departments, so it must be working satisfactorily! However, without checking the extent to which assessor OARs actually match up with ratings of on-the-job performance, the recruiter can never be sure of this point. We rest our case for validating even the most sophisticated AC and for evaluating the role that the interview plays in the assessment centre.

Reference letters

As the final stage in an organization's assessment of candidates, the reference request is normally sent to previous or current employers. It is perhaps more accurately placed within the induction phase of the selection process as shown in figure 2.1. It is advisable not to rely upon its contents too heavily since many references and testimonials are non-specific and broadly positive in their content (Anderson and Shackleton, 1986). The reference remains very popular, though, as indicated in figure 2.2, its principal value lies in checking the factual employment claims of the applicant and following-up any issues of concern outstanding from interview.

Phase IV: Induction

It is intriguing that some organizations spend so much time and resources on making their selection systems as objective and fair as possible and then almost totally neglect the induction of new appointees into their job roles. We will not labour this issue, but in some companies the authors have experienced a distinct perception that the 'duty of care' for the recruiter halts abruptly as soon as an offer of employment is placed in the post-out tray. Several home-truths need to be borne in mind at this stage:

- The candidate, not the organization, makes the final decision in the procedure – whether to accept the job offer or not. Notice also from figure 2.1 that the candidate also makes the initial decision whether or not to apply. To illustrate this point with some humour, case example 2.3 shows the effects of this aspect of decision making power in selection systems.
- The way the candidate is inducted into the organization may influence their levels of performance to the same degree to which this can be predicted by assessment techniques.
- The 'output' from the selection system should form the 'input' to the training system – training needs should thus be identified and acted upon.
- The transition of the appointee into their new job role will require personal adjustment and necessary support to maximize the job-person fit.

Case Example 2.3

Reversal of situational power at interview

It is usual in the further and higher education sectors for panel interviews to be used to select teachers, lecturers and researchers. Some readers may well have experienced this. The typical panel is comprised of one or two senior staff members from the department within which the vacancy falls; the chairperson usually from a position of authority higher up the organization hierarchy, one or two assorted characters from other departments, and the personnel officer in attendance to deal with terms and conditions of employment. Due to difficulties in coordinating the availability of all panel members, it is often the practice to interview all candidates at one sitting. Moreover, candidates are sometimes asked to remain until a decision has been reached and are then often informed of the outcome by the successful candidate being beckoned in first. If ever a procedure was designed to provoke anxiety in the poor interviewee, this is it!

In one such scenario known to the authors, the candidates neatly reversed this power distribution. All three candidates, having met up over lunch before the interview session, had agreed that the job was so unattractive that none of them wanted it but that they could all do with some interview experience! So the interviews went ahead as planned. Following all three interviews, the chairperson of the panel emerged to request their first choice appointee to come back in. She was offered the job but promptly turned it down. The chairperson once again emerged, this time looking somewhat crestfallen and asked the second-choice candidate to come back in. He in turn was offered the job but declined it. With embarrassment the chairperson came out for the third time and beckoned to the only remaining candidate to come back in. Again, the job offer was declined.

The interview panel were so distraught that they politely asked all three candidates to come in to the interview room together. The 30-minute session which followed was led by the interviewees each in turn letting the panel members know in no uncertain terms why the job offer was so singularly unattractive!

The Role of the Interview

As we have noted, many organizations have traditionally used the interview as a 'stand-alone' method of candidate assessment. That is, the interview has been used as the first and last stage of candidate assessment, only supplemented by the application form and followed-up only by the ubiquitous reference check. It is all too commonplace for recruiters to attempt to meet many diverse aims in the one solitary interview:

- To form an impression of candidate personality – i.e., using the interview as a surrogate personality test;
- To form an impression of candidate ability and intelligence – i.e., using the interview as a surrogate ability and intelligence test;
- To extrapolate from candidate behaviour at interview supposed on-the-job behaviour – i.e., using the interview as a surrogate work sample test.

To overload the interview – and the interviewer – in this way is a mistake. We have already outlined in this chapter the techniques of personality and ability testing and the use of work samples as proven methods of assessment which are capable of freeing-up the interview, and the interviewer, to concentrate upon domains for which this interpersonal situation is most suited. In essence, we are arguing that organizations often over-burden the interview by requiring it to fulfil the multiple functions of ability, personality and behaviour assessment, all of which should really be seen as independent but overlapping areas of assessment.

So, how should organizations be using the interview to maximize its contribution to their systems of selection? Work by Professor Peter Herriot of Sundridge Park Management Centre (1987) has suggested that the interview can be used in one of three ways:

- *Mutual preview* – to set up expectations for the selection process and to give candidates a realistic job preview (RJP).
- *Assessment* – to predict future on-the-job behaviour from preformulated interview questions.
- *Negotiation* – to reach agreement over outstanding issues contained in the contract of employment.

Table 2.3 summarizes these three strategies in terms of the stage in the selection system at which each approach is most suitable, the function of each type of interview, and the objectives of both the interviewer and interviewee. Let us consider each of these three functions in more detail.

Mutual preview

The interview provides an ideal forum in which both parties can obtain a mutual preview of the other. From the interviewer's viewpoint, they can meet the candidate face-to-face and provide them with information about the job in the form of a realistic job preview. This can be most useful in setting-up the candidates expectations regarding future stages of the selection procedure.

From the interviewee's perspective, a mutual preview interview gives the opportunity to visit the organization for the first time and to meet its representative – the interviewer. It is appropriate, then, that such an initial meeting should be informal and the agenda open to influence by both parties. This may sound a fairly radical proposal to those interviewers who hold the opinion that all candidates should be put through as stressful an experience as they can concoct! However, much research evidence supports the wisdom of using the initial interview as a mutual preview scenario (Anderson, 1992). Providing candidates with a dynamic, realistic job preview will enable them to perform a self-assessment for the job in question and to self-select out if they feel themselves to be unsuitable. After all, the candidate is surely in the best position to assess the suitability of the job for themselves in relation to their abilities and career objectives.

Assessment

We have argued that more attention should be given by recruiters to the exact assessment function performed by the interview. By partialing out personality and ability assessment through use of valid tests in these domains and by using work sample tests to indicate likely behaviour in the job situation, the interviewer is free to concentrate on reaching assessments of critical job behaviours. We consider this use of interviews in greater depth in chapters 3 and 4, so here we would simply note that good assessment interviews are built upon four cornerstones. They

● are *structured* around a standardized format;
● are based upon *detailed job analysis*; where
● questions relate to *critical job behaviours*; and
● candidate replies are *noted* or *rated* to infer possible *on-the-job behaviour* rather than candidate personality.

Table 2.3 Different functions of the interview

Interview function	Appropriate stage in selection procedure	Interview functioning	Interviewer objectives	Interviewee objectives
1 Mutual preview	Phase I/II Early stages of the selection procedure probably following the initial screening of written applications but preceeding the administration of main assessment techniques.	Informal, open-ended discussion to explain selection procedures and to offer career guidance counselling to the interviewee by providing a detailed and realistic job preview (RJP).	• To meet and 'set the scene' for the applicant • To advise applicants of the organizations selection procedure	• To establish what will be involved at each stage in the selection procedure • To visit the organization 'on-site' • To obtain a preview of the job to allow self-assessment and self-selection

2	Assessment	Phase II As one of a battery of candidate assessment techniques.	Formal, structured interaction guided by detailed job analysis and pre-formulated questioning strategy.	• To record answers to critical incident-type questions • To probe and feedback the results of other selection methods (particularly testing)	• To survive! • To obtain feedback and ensure accuracy of the results of other methods
3	Negotiation	Phase III Final stage of selection procedure immediately prior to, or after, an offer of employment has been made	Negotiation of outstanding points of difference, both interviewer and interviewee directed and led	• To ensure acceptance of the job offer • To facilitate job role transitions • To identify follow-up personnel procedures	• To discuss contractual and non-contractual terms and conditions • To facilitate job role transitions • To initiate the job change process

Again, the seasoned interviewer may regard such points as somewhat radical, arguing that they are unnecessary niceties which may be fine in theory but unrealistic in practice. This is far from correct since these cornerstones are perfectly feasible components of assessment interviews, which the more enlightened recruiting sections in HRM departments are already adopting.

Negotiation

The flexibility of the interview is perhaps its most endearing quality. It can be argued that this flexibility is best exploited by using the interview as a forum for negotiation between the parties. This is especially the case in the final stages of an organization's selection procedure where acceptance of the contract for employment needs to be secured by both sides. How might this be achieved? Undoubtedly, by this stage the candidate is aware of the strong possibility of their application being successful and should be told if a decision to appoint them has actually been reached. This leaves the negotiation interview free to deal with remaining issues such as exact start dates, notice periods required by their present employer, relocation procedures, training provisions, and so forth. The objective of the interviewer at this stage should be to ensure the candidate accepts any job offer and to ease the transition process by setting in motion any appropriate HRM procedures for relocation and training. Of course, interviewers need no reminder that the selection process is not complete until the candidate is actually settled into the job role and that their 'duty-of-care' therefore extends until this time!

Systems of Selection: Signing-off

Our aim in this chapter has been to establish a systems perspective of the role of the interview in selection. Far from being a standalone, all-encompassing assessment procedure, the interview is more modestly used to perform limited functions at different stages in the recruitment system. In 'setting the scene' for the following chapters which deal with these specific functions, we have also attempted to challenge some of the established custom and practice in industry regarding how selection interviews are typically used.

It may seem a little excessive to the reader for us to dedicate an entire chapter in a book on interviewing largely to other aspects of selection. However, we hope that it is clear by now that much can be gained from taking such a wider systems perspective of this process. In addition to the three fundamental assumptions of this approach detailed at the start of this chapter – selection systems as inter-related stages, chronological dependency, and assessment techniques as both predictors and affectors of behaviour – we would emphasize some final points to be born in mind by recruiters:

- *Built-in obsolescence*   As organizations change, so do the job roles within them. The faster the rate of organizational change, the more quickly will the selection system become obsolete. Therefore,
- *Validation is essential*   Regular checks that the system actually selects appropriate job incumbents need to be installed. Feedback from these validation checks should be used to modify the design of the system periodically as illustrated in figure 2.1.
- *Environmental jolts*   One state in the US has been reported recently as making it illegal to select on the grounds of physical attractiveness – so called 'uglyism'. This illustrates the fact that the legal context surrounding selection is changing constantly and organizations need to view selection as an 'open system' being influenced by such environ-mental developments.
- *Candidates as clients*   As we have noted, candidates make the first and last decisions in any selection system. The reputation of the organiza-tion as an employer, applicants' attitudes to work, and adverse publicity liable to dissuade candidates from applying, all need to be monitored carefully. Treating potential applicants in an unprofessional manner will only serve to persuade the better ones to look elsewhere and the poorer ones to accept any job offer only as a stop-gap measure.

Summary Propositions

1   Selection procedures are multi-stage systems comprising four inter-related sub-stages
    (a)   recruitment
    (b)   pre-screening
    (c)   candidate assessment
    (d)   induction
2   The interview is one of a range of candidate assessment methods, including cognitive tests, personality tests, work samples, and assess-ment centres
3   The interview can perform three distinct functions
    (a)   mutual preview

(b) assessment
(c) negotiation
4 Interviews 'fit' with other assessment methods in different ways depending upon the type of interview in question, but alternative techniques can alleviate some of the pressure on the interview
(a) psychometric tests of ability and personality
(b) work samples of on-the-job behaviour

Notes

1 See also D. Torrington and L. Hall (1989) *Personnel Management: A New Approach*, second edition (London: Prentice Hall International/ Institute of Personnel Management).
2 For further details see, for instance, M. Pearn and P. Kandola (1988) *Job Analysis: A Practical Guide for Managers* (London: IPM).
3 See P. Herriot (1984) *Down from the Ivory Tower: Graduates and Their Jobs* (Chichester: John Wiley).

References

Anderson, N. R. (1992) Eight Decades of Interview Research: a retrospective metareview and prospective commentary, *The European Work and Organizational Psychologist*, 2, 1–32.
Anderson, N. R. and Shackleton, V. J. (1986) Recruitment and Selection: a review of developments in the 1980's, *Personnel Review*, 15.4, 19–26.
Annastasi, A. (1988) *Psychological Testing* (New York: Macmillan).
Department of Employment (1971) *Glossary of Training Terms* (HMSO) second edition.
Feltham, R. (1988) Assessment Centre Decision Making: judgemental versus mechanical, *Journal of Occupational Psychology*, 61, 237–41.
Fletcher, C. (1982) Assessment Centres, in D. M. Davey and M. Harris (eds) *Judging People* (Maidenhead: McGraw-Hill).
Herriot, P. (1987) The Selection Interview, in P. Warr (ed.) *Psychology at Work* (Harmondsworth: Penguin).
Institute of Personnel Management (1991) *The IPM Recruitment Code*, London.
McHenry, R. (1981) The Selection Interview, in M. Argyle (ed.) *Social Skills and Work* (London: Methuen).
Munro Fraser, J. (1978) *Employment Interviewing* (London: MacDonald and Evans).
Rodger, A. (1952) *The Seven Point Plan*, National Institute for Industrial Psychology, Paper No. 1.

Shackleton, V. J. and Newell, S. (1991) Management Selection: A comparative survey of methods used in top British and French companies, *Journal of Occupational Psychology*, 64, 23–36.

Smith, M. (1986) Personnel Management, December.

Toplis, J., Dulewitz, V. and Fletcher, C. (1987) *Psychological Testing: A Practical Guide for Employers* (London: IPM).

3
Interview Efficiency: From Research Evidence to Practical Realities

'The interviewer must be a person able to break through the immediate behaviour of the candidate, which is likely to be determined very largely by the interview situation itself, and thus obtain real clues to his more basic qualities. Secondly, he must be capable of observing these clues accurately, quickly and comprehensively, and of forming a judgement unbiased by irrelevant considerations.'

Oldfield, *The Psychology of the Interview*, 1943

Interview Efficiency: Opening Shots

In chapter 2 we examined the ways in which interviews can contribute to accurate selection decision making. In this chapter our objective is more micro-analytical and specific in nature – to overview the applied research into interviews and interviewer decision making conducted over the last eighty years or so, and to draw practical conclusions from this published evidence.

In our experience there is no shortage of interviewers holding great faith in their own ability to assess others. The number of interviewers who believe that they can 'spot a good candidate as soon as they walk through the door' shows no signs of diminishing and, certainly, if there is any suggestion that interviews are in any way fallible, interviewers are convinced that it must be other peoples' interviews which are suspect, not their own! Unfortunately, contrary to these high levels of confidence in interviewers' decision making capacities there stands over eight decades of scientific research evidence. But just how pessimistic is the picture?.

Although, as will be seen, the research evidence is in some ways more encouraging than many HRM practitioners would believe, it highlights both weaknesses and strengths in the interview. It therefore points to good and bad practices in interviewing and suggests practical measures to maximize the interview's contribution to organizations' selection procedures.

Parry and Thrust

Since as long ago as 1915 (Scott, 1915) research studies have continued to uncover errors in the accuracy of interviewers' decisions and to cast doubt upon the value of the interview in employee selection (Anderson, 1992). An important point to note at the outset is that the focus of this research has been *the interviewer* and not *the interview*. In fact, there is no such thing as *the* interview – there are as many interviews as there are combinations of interviewers and interviewees. Faced with this reality, it should be emphasized that it was interviewers who were under scrutiny in these research studies. The implication is that careful attention needs to be paid to sources of potential error in interviewer decision making to ensure that interviewers are aware of these and to guard against their potentially detrimental effects.

We therefore need to be clear about what is meant by the term 'interview' before we can begin to answer the question whether or not interviews are effective as a method of personnel selection. The research into the interview is now very extensive, with the most recent review citing over 500 reports, articles and theses in this area (Anderson, 1992), but, broadly speaking, two distinct perspectives or theories of the interview are distinguishable:

- the 'objectivist-psychometric' perspective
- the 'subjectivist-social perception' perspective

1 The 'objectivist-psychometric' perspective Authors taking this view tend to conceive of the interview as a one-way information gathering technique – the interviewer being responsible for eliciting enough accurate information from the candidate upon which to make a selection decision. The candidate is often portrayed as a passive information provider whose sole function is to be there to give a representative sample of their behaviour from which the interviewer can then extrapolate to on-the-job behaviour. Although in this perspective the interviewer is seen as a personally-detached information gatherer and processor, he or she is also viewed as the primary source of error detracting from validity and reliability. In other words, if the interview goes astray, for whatever reason, the interviewer is to blame. The objectivist perspective has dominated research efforts in this area, despite concerns being voiced over this view of the interview as a one-way decision making process (Anderson, 1992). This has led to other researchers taking an entirely different theoretical perspective which can be termed the 'subjectivist-social perception' perspective.

2   *The 'subjectivist-social perception' perspective*   In this perspective the interview is seen as a two-way social encounter between the interviewer and the candidate. The participants are argued to 'negotiate' outcomes, whereby both make decisions over their future course of action. The interviewer's evaluation of the candidate is thus seen as only a by-product of this negotiation since the interview serves not only as a 'predictor' of suitability, but as an 'affector' of both parties' outcome decisions and future behaviour. Crucially, the interview is seen as effective, not merely to the extent to which the interviewer's ratings predict successful job performance, but to the extent to which this social encounter facilitates the negotiation of outcomes between the parties.

These two perspectives are discussed in detail in the academic literature, but it is important to note their impact here prior to reviewing the main research into interview efficiency and processes. This is especially the case since, as we have noted, through the research efforts of psychologists over the last eight decades, a huge body of studies into selection interviewer decision making has built up. The findings of these studies can be categorized under two headings:

- research into overall efficiency of interviewer decisions;
- research into specific errors in interviewer decision making.

Overall efficiency of interviewer decisions

Over the years many researchers have asked the question 'just how accurate are interviewers' decisions in predicting future job performance?' Fortunately, the volume of research evidence can be interpreted through recent developments in statistical methods for averaging out the findings of multiple research studies. The techniques of 'meta-analysis' and 'validity generalization' permit definitive statements to be made summarizing numerous separate research studies (Hunter and Hunter, 1984). Most important are the measures of interview validity and reliability, defined as follows:

- *Validity* – the extent to which an assessment technique *actually* measures what it purports to measure.
- *Reliability* – the extent to which an assessment technique measures *consistently*.

In the context of the interview, 'validity' refers to the ability of interviewers to predict the future job performance of candidates; 'reliability' to their ability to do so with consistency. For the interview to be effective, we are clearly looking to maximize both the validity and reliability of interviewer assessments.

The statistical technique usually applied to quantifying reliability and validity is the simple correlation coefficient. The correlation coefficient varies between –1.0 and +1.0, with zero as chance level prediction. We are thus seeking to obtain positive and fairly high correlations between interviewer ratings of candidates and subsequent ratings of their job performance (usually in the form of appraisal ratings or training evaluations). The scale range of the correlation coefficient is illustrated in figure 3.1.

So, how has the interview faired in terms of existing research into its validity and reliability? The answer is perhaps not what many personnel specialists would expect – the interview has proven to be quite valid and reliable overall. Figure 3.2 illustrates the findings of key review papers which have used meta-analysis techniques to average-out correlations across many studies in order to provide a general picture of interview validity and reliability. Meta-analysis as a statistical technique averages out the validity coefficients across many individual research studies, taking into account sources of variance between different studies.

Remember that it is rare to obtain correlation coefficients of more than about 0.5 or 0.6 in real-life selection situations, mainly because so many other factors which cannot be foreseen at interview impinge upon subsequent job performance. Figure 3.2 shows recent findings are much more supportive of the interview than many recruiters may believe. Structured interviews held on average predictive validity of 0.62 in the most recent meta-analysis (Wiesner and Cronshaw, 1988), twice that of unstructured interviews. Structured

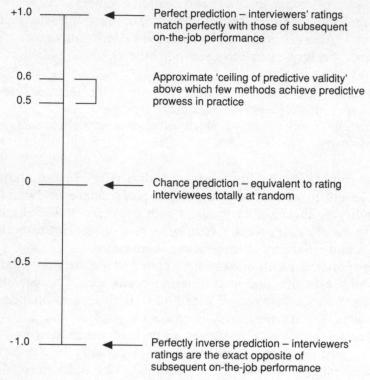

Figure 3.1   Correlation coefficients in selection.

interviews were also more reliable (0.85 compared to 0.61 for un-structured), although few major differences emerged between one-to-one and panel interviews. These and other findings indicate five key points on overall interview efficiency:

• Interviews can be much more accurate than many recruiters may believe;
• Structured interviews are more valid and reliable than unstructured interviews;
• Interviews are significantly more accurate if based upon detailed job analysis techniques;
• The interview is an appropriate and fairly reliable method for assessing job-relevant social skills;
• Interviewer accuracy varies and recruitment decisions should always be validated.

Let us consider briefly each of these points in turn.

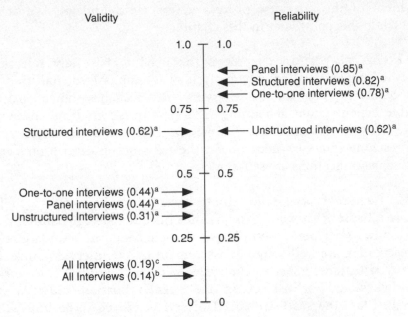

Validity   Reliability

- 1.0 — 1.0
- ← Panel interviews (0.85)[a]
- ← Structured interviews (0.82)[a]
- ← One-to-one interviews (0.78)[a]
- 0.75 — 0.75
- Structured interviews (0.62)[a] →   ← Unstructured interviews (0.62)[a]
- 0.5 — 0.5
- One-to-one interviews (0.44)[a] →
- Panel interviews (0.44)[a] →
- Unstructured Interviews (0.31)[a] →
- 0.25 — 0.25
- All Interviews (0.19)[c] →
- All Interviews (0.14)[b] →
- 0 — 0

Figure 3.2 How valid and reliable is the selection interview?
Sources (a) W. H. Wiesner and S. F. Cronshaw, *Journal of Occupational Psychology*, 61 (1988), pp. 275–290, (b) J. E. Hunter and R. G. Hunter, *Psychological Bulletin*, 96 (1984), pp. 72–98, (c) R. R. Reilly and G. T. Chao, *Personnel Psychology*, 35 (1982), pp. 1–62.

1 *Interview accuracy* Existing folklore among practising recruiters is that interviews are thought to be quite reasonable predictors of job performance, although many recruiters will have some knowledge of interview research which casts doubt upon aspects of the interview as a selection tool. The recent evidence supports the belief that the interview is a comparatively accurate method of assessment. Referring back to figure 2.2 in chapter 2, the interview clearly holds its own against other candidate assessment techniques, so long as it is *structured* and based upon detailed *job analysis* techniques.

2 *Structured interviews* The research evidence is unequivocal – structured interviews built around a preplanned format are demonstrably more valid than unstructured, non-directed conversations (Wiesner and Cronshaw, 1988). There is little doubt, then, that for *assessment purposes* interviewers should be working to preplanned schedules which at least, to some extent, guide and standardize the

content of the interview process across all candidates. We shall return to this point later in this chapter.

3   *Job analysis*   In chapter 2 the need to base any selection method upon detailed job analysis was emphasized and this is especially the case for the interview. Research has shown quantifiable benefits from generating interview questions from in-depth job analysis (Wiesner and Cronshaw, 1988), and the advantages of reaching interview decision on the basis of job descriptions and person specifications are self-evident.

4   *Candidate social skills*   Interviewers have been found to be more reliable at assessing two qualities in candidates: sociability and likeability (Wagner, 1949). These two elements of candidate self-presentation are well-suited to assessment by the interview since, in many situations, effective interview behaviour replicates essential job behaviour. For instance, in one recent validation study (Arvey, et al., 1987) the semi-structured interview proved to be unusually accurate at predicting success in sales positions (interviewers' ratings correlated with supervisors' performance ratings at 0.42 after one year in the job). It was clear that the types of social skills and skills of interpersonal persuasion needed at interview replicated those needed on-the-job itself. The interview situation can therefore be exploited to assess candidates' self-presentation skills and can appropriately be utilized by recruiters in this way.

5   *Validation*   Are some interviewers better than others? Wide variations in the accuracy of individual interviewers have been reported in several studies (Anderson, 1992), but conclusive evidence regarding the factors influencing these differences has proved hard to uncover. The important implication is that recruiters should validate their own interview decisions against subsequent ratings of candidates' performance on-the-job.

Organizations implementing these measures to maximize the predictive efficiency of the interview stand to benefit substantially from more carefully considered and accurate interview decisions. Unfortunately, current practice in many organizations falls well short of these standards. In many cases interviews are still being conducted without prior job analysis and with a lack of structure or assessment objectives. Under these circumstances interviewer decisions are likely to be inaccurate and open to a number of errors highlighted in research on the interview. It is to this process of interviewer decision making and to these pitfalls inherent in the process that we now turn.

Errors in interviewer decision making

This second category of interview research has illustrated a number of errors or dysfunctions that interviewers are prone to in the way that they interpret information on candidates. Figure 3.3 shows the stages through which an interviewer is likely to progress to reach a decision on each candidate.

This figure models the decision making process, asserting that three major sources of information are available to the interviewer:

- Documented biographical information (i.e., application form or CV);
- Candidate verbal behaviour at interview (i.e., replies to questions);
- Candidate non-verbal behaviour at interview (i.e., body language).

Candidate verbal behaviour can be classified by 'content', elements of the reply itself; and by 'process', the way the reply is affected by speech characteristics. The candidate's non-verbal behaviour or body language can be considered in two ways. First, 'static' cues which remain unchanged for the duration of the interview, including physical appearance, and second, 'dynamic' constantly changing cues including patterns of eye contact, facial expressions and gestures.

In most interviews these three sources of information will constitute the 'input data' to the interviewer's decision making process. But how does the interviewer interpret and combine all these data into a final selection decision? Based upon previous research (Anderson, 1988), the model proposes four stages in interviewer impression formation:

- recognition
- translation
- assimilation
- justification

The initial stage is that of *recognizing* the relevance of a piece of information. Due to the mass of information presented to the interviewer, many pieces of data are likely to pass unnoticed.

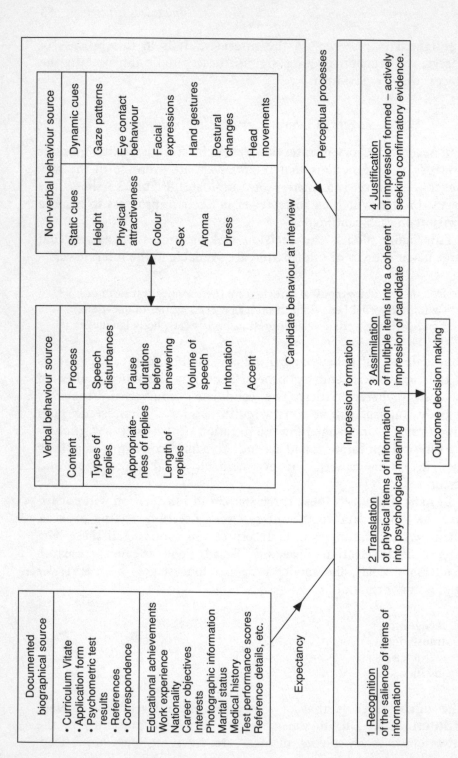

Figure 3.3 A cognitive-social model of interviewer decision making.

Nonetheless, many items of information will be recognized as important and then *translated* into psychological meaning as the second stage of impression formation. For instance, an interviewer listening to a candidate describing her ability to work long hours in a previous job may well infer both commitment and a conscientious approach to work. The third stage of *assimilation* occurs when the interviewer 'pieces the picture together' into a coherent whole. Using our hypothetical example, the interviewer, upon receiving a letter of reference on this candidate commending her dedication and motivation, may well assimilate this data, together with the interview impressions, into a highly positive overall picture. This can be followed by the interviewer seeking information to confirm this impression and to *justify* their decision. For example, the interviewer may browse through the candidate's application form again searching for information to confirm this impression of a conscientious, diligent worker.

In reality, the process of interviewer decision making is a highly complex activity which involves integrating multiple data from these main sources into a coherent, justifiable whole, while simultaneously managing the social interaction with the candidate. So our model simplifies this process but does so intentionally to help visualize the stages involved in obtaining, interpreting, and integrating candidate data from multiple sources to arrive at an overall impression and outcome decision.

Linking the sources of data with this process of impression formation are what we have termed *expectancy processes* and *perceptual processes*. Expectancy is where an interviewer forms a range of impressions on the candidate soley on the basis of documented biographical data. We consider this process as a potential error in the following section of this chapter.

Much research has been conducted into interviewer perceptual processes and it is in this area that many of the pitfalls in interviewer decision making have been uncovered. The list of these potential errors is not short – at least twelve major dysfunctions have repeatedly been found across studies in several countries. These are:

- Expectancy effect
- Confirmatory information seeking bias
- Primacy effect
- Stereotyping and prototyping

- Halo/horns effect
- Contrast and quota effect
- Negative information bias
- Similar-to-me effect
- Personal liking bias
- Information overload and selective attention
- Fundamental attribution error
- Temporal extension

1   *Expectancy effect – Interviewers form an expectancy of the candidate based on documented biographical information which strongly affects their final decision*   Many studies have shown the tendency for interviewers to generate either positive or negative expectancies from application form details and for their decisions to follow these expectations (Wareing and Stockdale, 1987). As we illustrate in case example 3.1, expectancy effect can easily set up either an upward or downward spiral prior to even meeting the candidate.

Case Example 3.1

Expectancy effect

Brief

You are the graduate recruitment officer for a multinational knitware manufacturer. Having advertised in a national student vacancies newsletter, you have received the following application for a vacancy in the Materials Research and Development Division.

Application Form

Surname	Perkinson-Smythe
First names	James Perrigrine
Date of birth	10.12.73
Term address	Queens College University of Cambridge
Place of birth	Esher, Surrey
Nationality	English

Secondary education	Harrow Boys School 9 'O Levels 3 'A' Levels (physics, mathematics, chemistry, All at Grade 'A')
University education	BSc Applied Physics, Expected Degree – First Class Honours with Distinction (All first and second year examination results at this level)
Final year project	'Materials production and processing techniques in advanced semi-synthetic knitware'
Awards/prizes	Awarded 'Student of exceptional merit' awards for first and second year studies. Awarded university Full Colours for captaining the university rugby team to National Championship 1992/93. Awarded vice-captain of the university lacrosse team.
Leisure activities	Rugby, lacrosse, hockey, cycling. Student counsellor in the welfare office one afternoon each weekend. Telephone counsellor for Cambridge 'ChildLine' service two nights per week (10 pm – 6.30 am). Cycling from Cambridge to Delhi to raise sponsorship for the Cancer Research Campaign: July/August following final examinations.
Supporting statement	May I add some final comments to my application? It is important for my own peace of mind to be totally committed to all activities I am involved with, be they work or leisure. My training as a ChildLine counsellor has really improved my social skills and, during quiet periods, it has allowed me to finish off project work and do exam revision. For my summer holiday this year I am planning a 9–week

sponsored cycle ride, from Cambridge to Delhi, in aid of Cancer Research. This will be a demanding task, but I have pledges amounting to £7000 in sponsorship from local industry and residents if I succeed.

Respectfully yours

Jim P-Smythe

Questions

1   What impressions of this candidate do you have?
2   If you noted your impressions of the candidate without reading his leisure activities, would they be substantially different?
3   Did you feel any information on the candidate was conflictual, or merely your interpretation of the factual data?
4   What questions would you wish to ask him at interview?

2   *Confirmatory information seeking bias – Interviewers actively seek information to confirm their initial impressions*   Closely linked to expectancy effect is confirmatory information seeking bias. Research indicates that interviewers ask questions designed to elicit information confirming their initial impressions (Macon and Dipboye, 1988). The interview can therefore become a self-fulfilling prophesy with the interviewer only collecting and attending to information which supports their snap judgements.

3   *Primacy effect – Interviewers form impressions of candidates very early on in the interview*   A common misinterpretation of the research is that interviewers *make decisions* on candidates very early on, usually in the first four minutes of the interview. The original findings giving rise to this belief emerged from research conducted at McGill University, Canada in the 1950s under the direction of the late Professor Edward Webster (Webster, 1964). More recent studies have contradicted this early finding (Anderson, 1992) and opinion remains divided over whether interviewers reach outcome decisions in the first few minutes of the interview. There is, however, substantially clear evidence showing that interviewers are prone to primacy effect in two other ways:

● Interviewers tend to form lasting impressions of *candidate personality* very early on (Anderson, 1988).
● Interviewers are more influenced by information emerging early in the interview compared with later information (Webster, 1964).

One pitfall found by research is that interviewers tend to make snap judgements on the *candidate's personality* and that these initial impressions are highly resistant to change (Anderson and Shackleton, 1990). The second finding, that early information carries greater weight than later information, allies with the results of research into expectancy effect and confirmatory information seeking bias. Clearly, if allowed to, interviewer decision making can deteriorate into a process of merely attempting to confirm snap judgements on candidates.

4 *Stereotyping and prototyping – Interviewers possess notions of stereotypical and prototypical ideal job holders and screen candidates against these notions* Stereotyping occurs where a characteristic, assumed by the interviewer to be held by a particular group, is ascribed to all individuals within that group. Stereotyping on the basis of race, gender, physique or other group membership characteristics can not only be highly erroneous and discriminatory, but also possibly illegal (see chapter 8). Interviewers should therefore be consciously guarding against this bias.

Prototyping is where interviewers believe that there is an ideal personality type regardless of the job function being recruited for. This effect has been found to exist in graduate selection, for instance, where interviewers were seeing large numbers of applicants for fundamentally different job functions, but screening using an overall 'ideal-type' prototype (Anderson and Shackleton, 1990).

5 *Halo/horns effect – Interviewers interpret information and rate candidates in either a generally positive or generally negative manner* A good indication of halo/horns effect is where an interviewer has rated all factors on the interviewee assessment form either universally favourably or universally unfavourably. Of course, the ratings may follow on from the interviewer's overall decision: the accepted candidate being rated favourably on all factors, the rejected candidate unfavourably on all factors. Ironically, the authors have spoken with interviewers who firmly believed this was required of them by their organizations!

6 *Contrast and quota effect – Interviewers' decisions are affected by decisions on earlier candidates and pre-set employment quotas* A long-standing research finding is that the interviewer's decision on the current candidate is influenced both by decisions on preceding candidates, and by employment quotas set by the organization (Harris, 1989). Case example 3.2 suggests one possible scenario where contrast effect may be occurring.

Case Example 3.2

Contrast and quota effect in selection

Susan Carpenter, personnel manager for a medium-sized light engin-eering firm, is interviewing for six clerical vacancies in the accounts department. A display advertisement in the local press attracted 30 applicants who have been screened down to 18 interviewees to be seen by Susan Carpenter over three days. The first two days go well and Susan has rated five applicants as 'strong possibilities' with a sixth being rated a 'borderline reserve'. Six others have been rejected as unsuitable for various reasons.

Questions

1 What chances do applicants being seen by Susan Carpenter on her third day of interviews have of being selected?
2 Should Susan Carpenter consider overturning any of her earlier decisions?
3 What errors in interviewer decision making may render her reluctant to do so?

One method of minimizing contrast effect is for the interviewer to complete individual interviewee assessments but to withhold outcome decisions until all candidates have been seen. From both the organization's perspective of achieving accurate selection de-cisions and from the candidate's perspective of being given a fair opportunity to present themselves, this is one method to combat contrast and quota effect.

7 *Negative information bias – Interviewers' decisions are influenced significantly more by negative information than by positive information* Over the years many studies have concluded that candidate infor-mation which carries negative connotations affects interviewers

much more than positive information (Webster, 1964). The practical realities of organizational life may explain why this is so. A candidate who is appointed but proves to be a poor job performer is visible to the interviewer's peers and so he or she may well receive negative feedback on an 'incorrect' selection decision. On the other hand, rejected interviewees who would have made excellent job incumbents are never seen by the recruiter's peers. If allowed to, the interview can become a search for an excuse to reject each particular candidate. To guard against this bias, interviewers should undoubtedly be encouraged to elicit both negative and positive details from all candidates and to weigh up their decisions on the balance of both types of information. From the opposing perspective of the interviewee, it is doubtless advisable for candidates to avoid imparting negative information at any stage during the interview process, and certainly never during the opening few minutes!

8 *Similar-to-me effect – Interviewers select candidates similar to themselves in biographical background, personality and attitudes* Otherwise known as the 'clone syndrome', similar-to-me effect biases interviewers' evaluations in favour of candidates with similar educational backgrounds, biographical details, personality and attitudes (Anderson and Shackleton, 1990). The potential hazard, of course, is that in the long-term an organization may become staffed by a homogeneous group of like-minded individuals who are unable to bring a diversity of perspectives and attitudes to bear on issues facing the organization.

9 *Personal liking bias – Interviewers favour candidates whom they like personally* A pervasive bias found in interview studies is that interviewers' decisions as to employability are strongly influenced by their personal liking for candidates. One researcher concludes:

> Perhaps a common stereotype of the good interviewer is that of the dispassionate observer who remains emotionally detached while carefully evaluating each candidates' strengths and weaknesses in terms of his potential job performance. The research results suggest that this is the exception rather than the rule[14]. (Keenan, 1977, p. 281)

Other research supports Keenan's assertion and perhaps many interviewers would grudgingly admit that personal liking bias may have a lot to do with their final accept or reject decisions.

10   *Information overload and selective attention – Interviewers have too much information to cope with and so attend to only a fraction of the available data*   There is evidence to show that interviewers are operating under conditions of 'information overload' and as a result they 'selectively attend' to only some of the data within the total flow of information (Anderson, 1992; Webster, 1964; Harris, 1989). Perhaps many interviewers would agree intuitively with this finding and certainly the authors have been told on countless occasions by practising interviewers of the complexity of simultaneously searching for and interpreting information during the interview. The inference is that our neat, linear information processing model presented in figure 3.4 flatters interviewers' actual cognitive strategies – more realistically they are probably striving to cope as best they can under an inordinate load of information, forming judgements on only a fraction of the data available to them.

11   *Fundamental attribution error – Interviewers incorrectly attribute the cause of candidate behaviour at interview to their personality rather than to situational constraints and demands*   'Fundamental attribution error' (Herriot, 1989) is where an interviewer erroneously ascribes or attributes candidate behaviour to facets of their personality rather than to the actual cause of their behaviour – the stressful situation of the interview itself. Referring back to issues of selection systems discussed in chapter 2, the reader will recall that we cautioned against using unstructured impressions of candidate behaviour to infer on-the-job behaviour. Of course, the interviewer has no real way of discovering whether the interviewee's behaviour is caused by their underlying personality or by the stressful situation of the interview itself. It is precisely because of this uncertainty that such inferences should be made only with great care by interviewers. Case example 3.3 illustrates one way in which fundamental attribution error may occur at interview.

Case Example 3.3

Fundamental attribution error

The computer services manager, Jane Rutland, is in the midst of interviewing a nervous candidate for the post of computer analyst. She realized early on that the candidate was anxious because of several tell-tale signs: fidgeting and frequent changes in seating

position, not looking her in the eye, short abrupt answers to questions, and most off-putting of all – constantly clicking a retractable
ball-point pen clutched in his left hand. Remembering her interviewer training and similar behaviour by an ex-boyfriend several
years earlier, Jane Rutland makes allowances for these initial
impressions reasoning that these behaviours are due to 'interview
nerves'. However, this self-presentation style continues throughout
the entire 45-minute interview despite Jane's relaxing manner and
gentle questioning. Jane Rutland eventually decides that these behaviours indicate certain personality traits in the candidate.

Questions

1 What traits would you, the reader, attribute to the applicant?
2 Would these necessarily be disadvantageous in the job of systems
  analyst?
3 Has Jane Rutland been unfair to this interviewee?

12 *Temporal extension – Interviewers 'temporally extend' candidate
behaviour at interview to infer longer term emotional states and personality
traits* The final error uncovered by interview research can be
termed 'temporal extension' and occurs where the interviewer
wrongly extrapolates from candidate behaviour to infer firstly mood/
emotional states, and secondly, longer-term dispositional traits of
personality (Harris, 1989). Figure 3.4 illustrates this process and
again shows the dangers of reading too much into interviewee
behaviour.

From Research to Reality: Combating Errors in
Decision Making

Having studied this array of potential errors in interviewer decision
making, the reader will be forgiven for reaching the conclusion that
interviews should play no part in any organization's selection
procedure! The range of possible pitfalls is undeniably extensive
and should shake the faith of even the most hard-bitten and self-
confident of interviewers. On the other hand, many lessons can be
learnt from these research findings. The major implications of these
studies lie in relation to how the interview is used in staff selection.

The paramount issue of concern for recruiters is the purpose
which the interview is intended to serve in selection. Why interview

Level 1: Superficial behaviour

Example

Candidate displays frequent smiling and laughing, both in immediate response to the interviewer and while answering open-ended questions

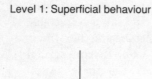

Level 2: Inference to state

Interviewer infers lack of anxiety, happiness, and that the candidate is at ease in this social encounter

Level 3: Inference to traits

Interviewer infers several personality traits:
• outgoing, extrovert
• happy-go-lucky
• self-confident in social situations
• highly positive self-image held by the candidate
• developed sense of humour, etc.

Figure 3.4   Temporal extension in inferring personality from behaviour.

at all given this morass of potential inaccuracies? The answer is that interviews have the potential for collecting certain types of information essential to an accurate two-way selection decision that other selection techniques are unsuited to collecting.

In chapter 2 we highlighted three distinct types of interview conducted at different stages in the selection system – mutual preview, assessment, and negotiation. Having now examined the research evidence on interviewer decision making, we can make some pragmatic recommendations on the use of these different types of interview in recruitment. Table 3.1 summarizes our recommendations, which we come on to develop in greater depth in chapters 4 and 5.

Before concluding this review of the implications of the research evidence for interviewing in practice, it is only reasonable that we look briefly at the 'other side of the coin', so to speak, by commenting on how *interviewees* have been found to reach decisions on organizations as potential employers.

Curioser and curioser: Candidate decision making

How do candidates form impressions of organizations during selection procedures? Is the interview particularly influential on the

candidate's decision making process as it is often the only opportunity for them to 'see the organization from the inside'? What do
interviewees infer from interviewer behaviour? And, ultimately, what
persuades candidates to accept or reject an offer of employment?

These questions, and many others besides, spring immediately
to mind when considering the vexed issue of how candidates infer
organizational characteristics from their experiences at interview
and how they then assimilate these into their outcome decisions
to accept or reject an offer of employment. Distilling the research
findings in this area, five main points arise:

- Perceived interviewer personableness, competence and informativeness
  influence the likelihood of candidates accepting any offer of employment (Harris, 1989);
- Interviewer behaviours carry greater weight than either administrative procedures or assessment methods in candidate decision making
  (Harris, 1989; Harris and Fink, 1987);
- Candidates prefer to trust informal sources of information on organizations, including friends, relatives and word-of-mouth, rather than
  informal sources (Harris, 1989);
- Career information given by organizations may influence candidates
  intentions to apply in the first instance (Harris, 1989);
- A few researchers even argue that the interviewer is seen as the
  representative of the organization, embodying all its virtues and
  drawbacks (Herriot, 1989).

Despite these key findings there is much less research into applicant
decision making than into interviewer decision making. Even so,
these points again highlight that the interview is a two-way process
with both parties assessing each other in an attempt to predict how
satisfactory any future work relationship would turn out to be. In
times of labour shortage, or where candidates have rare and valued
expertise and so may have offers from more than one potential
employer, it is clear that interviewer behaviours can influence the
calibre of entrants to the organization.

Interview efficiency: Parting shots

This chapter has now come full circle – from pointing out initially
the likely inefficiency of the selection interview as commonly practised, to identifying the major sources of error in interviewer
decision making which create such inaccuracy, and, in conclusion,
to examining decision making from the perspective of the candidate.

Table 3.1 Practical recommendations for interview usage

Interview stage	Ensure	Avoid	Importance of validity and reliability
Mutual preview	• Informality • Freedom for mutual information exchange • Candidate asks questions and obtains relevant information	• Snap judgements on the candidates suitability • Fundamental attribution error-behaviour may well be situation-specific • Over-selling the organization even in a 'sellers' labour market	• Only of importance from the candidate's point of view as the aim is to facilitate their self-evaluation • Concerns of validity and reliability from the organization's perspective less important at this stage
Assessment	• Based upon detailed job analysis and a structured approach • Critical dimensions of job performance are predicted by appropriate interview questions • Some flexibility is retained to follow up emergent issues	• Unstructured 'friendly chats' as assessment interviews • Inferring too much too quickly • Exploiting your power as interviewer over the candidate • Other biases discussed in this chapter	• Of crucial importance • Validity coefficients in excess of 0.4 and reliability coefficients above 0.8 are reasonable aims

Negotiation

- The best candidates
  accept employment offers,
  although beware again of
  over-selling
- Candidates' expectations
  of the induction period are
  realistic
- Any outstanding queries
  on both sides are resolved
  satisfactorily

- Excessive concessions to
  strong candidates – if they
  have come this far they
  probably want the job
  regardless
- Excessively tough
  bargaining – you may
  undermine long-term
  goodwill

- Exploring the bilateral
  contract of work of greater
  importance than 'pure'
  validity of interviewer
  assessment
- Reliability an unsuitable
  measure as each
  negotiation interview will
  be different

For sure, the interview is not a perfect and infallible method but, then, neither are many interviewers! But being cognisant of the potential pitfalls in impression formation and decision making revealed by research is an important first step to becoming a skilled and effective interviewer. While the interview has received considerable 'bad press' by researchers and practitioners over the years, the more recent findings are far less pessimistic. Utilized properly, depending upon its exact purpose, the interview emerges as a valid and reliable tool in candidate assessment. Moreover, its flexibility to act as a medium for mutual preview or as a final-stage forum for negotiation between the parties, renders the interview more useful in selection than narrowly focused definitions of validity and reliability can convey. As one practising interviewer once demanded of one of the authors – 'tell me in one sentence how I should interview given these eighty years of international research findings!' The reply? 'Interview effectiveness depends upon how it is used, by whom, and to what ends its outcomes are put.'

Summary Propositions

1 The interview is more valid and reliable than many personnel practitioners believe.
2 Assessment interviews based upon detailed job analysis and using a structured format are significantly more valid and reliable than unstructured interviews.
3 Interviewers are the major source of error, being prone to a variety of dysfunctions in their information processing strategies.
4 Interviewer expectations of the candidate, coupled with earlier information carrying greater weight than information emerging later in the interview, may set up a self-fulfilling prophesy.
5 Interviewers may experience 'information overload' during the interview and may attempt to cope by 'selectively attending to' only a fraction of the available data.
6 The flexibility of the interview to fulfil other purposes, including mutual preview and negotiation functions, renders measures of validity and reliability less paramount in these purposes.

References

Anderson, N. R. (1988) *Interviewer Impression Formation and Decision Making in the Graduate Selection Interview: A theoretical and Empirical Analysis.* Unpublished PhD thesis, University of Aston, UK.

Anderson, N. R. (1992) Eight Decades of Employment Interview Research: a retrospective meta-review and prospective commentary, *The European Work and Organizational Psychologist*, 2, 1–32.

Anderson, N. R. and Shackleton, V. J. (1990) Decision Making in the Graduate Selection Interview: a field study, *Journal of Occupational Psychology*, 63, 63–6.

Arvey, R. D. Miller, H. E., Gould, R. and Burch, P. (1987) Interview Validity for Selecting Sales Clerks, *Personnel Psychology*, 40, 1–12.

Harris, M. M. (1989) Reconsidering the Employment Interview: a review of recent literature and suggestions for future research, *Personnel Psychology*, 42, 691–726.

Harris, M. M. and Fink, L. S. (1987) A Field Study of Applicant Reactions to Employment Opportunities: does the recruiter make a difference? *Personnel Psychology*, 40, 765–84.

Herriot, P. (1989) Attribution Theory and Interview Decisions, in R. W. Eder & G. R. Ferris (eds) *The Employment Interview: Theory, Research and Practice* (Newbury: Sage).

Hunter, J. E. and Hunter, R. F. (1984) Validity and Utility of Alternate Predictors of Job Performance, *Psychological Bulletin*, 96, 72–98.

Keenan, A. (1977) Some Relationships Between Interviewers' Personal Feelings about Candidates and Their General Evaluation of Them, *Journal of Occupational Psychology*, 50, 275–83.

Macon, T. H. and Dipboye, R. L. (1988) The Effects of Interviewers Initial Impressions on Information Gathering, *Organizational Behavior and Human Decision Processes*, 42, 364–87.

Oldfield, R. C. (1943) *The Psychology of the Interview* (London: Methuen).

Scott, E. D. (1915) Scientific Selection of Salesmen, *Advertising and Selling Magazine*, October.

Wagner, R. (1949) The Employment Interview: a critical summary, *Personnel Psychology*, 2, 17–46.

Wareing, R. and Stockdale, J. (1987) Decision Making in the Promotion Interview: an empirical study, *Personnel Review*, 16, 4.

Webster, E. C. (1964) *Decision making in the Employment Interview* (Quebec: Eagle Publishing Co. Ltd).

Wiesner, W. H. and Cronshaw, S. F. (1988) A Meta-analytic Investigation of the Impact of Interview Format and Degree of Structure on the Validity of the Employment Interview, *Journal of Occupational Psychology*, 61, 275–90.

4

Interview Structures
and Formats

'There are a number of areas in which the potential of the interview cannot be surpassed by other selection methods ... in an interview some assessment can be made of matters that cannot be approached in any other way.'

Torrington and Hall, *Personnel Management: A New Approach*, 1987

Interview Structures: Tight or Loose?

The first author of this book well remembers one interviewer's solution to structuring his interviews. This consisted of a list of around forty largely unrelated questions which were asked verbatim and in exactly the same order regardless of candidates' replies! Indeed, candidates' answers appeared to exert no influence whatsoever on him and were lost in this rapid-fire, undeviating interrogation. Final decisions seemed to be determined to a large extent by the fluency of candidates' replies regardless of the actual contents!

This anecdote, although admittedly a rather extreme example of over-structured interviewing, highlights a perennial problem in employee selection – just how structured and preplanned should interviews be?

In this chapter we examine this issue by reflecting further on the different types of interview in use at the present time and by evaluating their contribution to selection decision making. Comparing and contrasting these different types of interview we conclude that there *is* an appropriate structure for every interview. Just how structured depends on the circumstances involved.

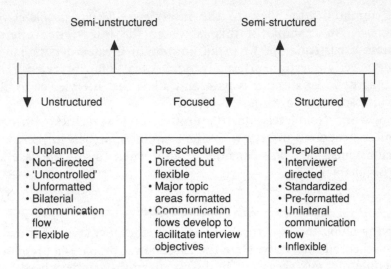

Figure 4.1 The structural continuum.

The Structural Continuum

So, what is meant by the term 'interview structure'? It can be argued that any interview can be placed at some point along the 'structural continuum' illustrated in figure 4.1.

The continuum ranges from totally *unstructured*, through *focused* at the mid-point, to totally *structured* at the other extreme. Let us consider each type of interview in turn.

Unstructured interviews

A totally unstructured interview is the hallmark of an unskilled interviewer. No objectives are set, no plans laid down, and as a result the interviewer is liable to lose any semblance of control over the interaction. Unfortunately, this scenario is all to commonplace, as many interviewees will readily testify. The unstructured interview is doubly damaging. Not only is it an inefficient selection method, but it is apt to create a negative impression of the organization with candidates who then share their experience with others.

The completely unstructured interview needs to be distinguished from the semi-unstructured interview which can contribute positively in employee selection. Here, only a moderate degree of structure is imposed so that major interviewer objectives are established beforehand. The interviewer is willing to relinquish control over the communication flow to the interviewee *if this facilitates these objectives*. An example of this is where the interviewee offers to explain a particular point in an answer in greater detail than the interviewer's question originally demanded. The interviewer may then agree to go along this path and allow the interviewee to 'lead' the interaction for a while.

So, while completely unstructured interviews achieve little, the semi-unstructured interview can be a useful approach in the correct circumstances. We will consider exactly when this is the case later in this chapter.

Focused interviews

Moving along the structural continuum, the next style of interview is the focused interview. Here the interviewer prepares a preplanned schedule of topic areas but builds in flexibility under these broad headings for specific replies to be followed-up and probed into. These properties make the focused interview most useful since it contains elements of both preplanning and flexibility. It also exploits fully the skills of 'funnelling', probing, and summarizing, described in chapter 6 as core interviewing skills. Importantly, the balance between preplanned questioning and spontaneous reactions by the interviewer must be struck and adhered to throughout the duration of the interview.

Structured interviews

In recent years several developments have occurred in structured interview techniques. These developments have been driven by the desire of occupational psychologists to improve the accuracy of unstructured interviews to equal that of tests and assessment centres (Eder and Ferris, 1989) (see figure 2.4 in chapter 2). We come on to review several of these techniques later in this chapter, but it is important to note at this stage the main similarities between many types of structured interview, i.e.:

- The interaction is standardized as much as possible; with
- all candidates being asked the same series of questions;
- replies are rated by the interviewer; usually
- on pre-formatted and behaviourally-anchored rating scales; whereby
- dimensions for rating are derived from critical aspects of on-the-job behaviour.

Interview structure

Interview functions	Unstructured	Focused	Structured
Mutual preview	(Semi-unstructured) 0	*	X
Assessment	X	0	*
Negotiation	(Semi-unstructured) *	0	X

Key: * = most suitable   0 = possibly suitable   X = unsuitable

Figure 4.2   Appropriate degrees of structure for different interviews.

Appropriate Degrees of Structure

How structured should an interview be? The answer is, of course, that it all depends on the circumstances involved. Returning to the three functions of the interview described in chapters 2 and 3 – mutual preview, assessment, and negotiation – we can now determine appropriate degrees of structure in each case. Figure 4.2 summarizes the recommended degree of structure.

The *mutual preview interview* has the aim of establishing initial contact between the parties and facilitating candidate self-selection. It is most appropriately structured as a focused interview or possibly as a semi-structured interview. This allows flexibility for the interviewer to react to the interviewee's objectives but also imposes sufficient structure to ensure that the interviewer's aims are also met.

The *assessment interview*, on the other hand, is best established on a highly structured basis since this maximizes predictive efficiency.[1] In some circumstances it may be justifiable to reduce the degree of structure to use a focused interview for assessment purposes. For instance, in senior managerial appointments the highly structured interview, if mostly one way, may cause offence to the applicant who expects to 'negotiate' his or her position at all points in the recruitment procedure.

Finally, the *negotiation interview*, used to tie up any loose ends, at the conclusion of the selection process, is most appropriately conducted as a semi-unstructured type of interview. The interviewer is unaware of many content areas for discussion since these will be brought into the interaction by the interviewee. A considerable degree of flexibility for the interviewer to respond is therefore a prerequisite for negotiation interviews, which therefore dictates the use of a semi-unstructured format. Only rarely will the interviewer have sufficient warning of likely content to permit the use of a focused interview but, if this is the case, then undoubtedly the interviewer should plan on this basis.

To summarize the issue of appropriate degrees of structure, the response is that 'it all depends'. All other things being equal, mutual preview interviews are most appropriately conducted with a focused structure, assessment interviews on a highly structured basis, and final-stage negotiation interviews using a semi-unstructured approach.

Interview Formats: Common Types of Design

Having examined the ideal relationship between interview structure and function, it is necessary to contrast these prescriptions with interview formats in common usage. Two important points to note at the outset are that:

- Many interviews currently in widespread use are, in fact, focused biographical interviews (Millar, Crute and Hargie, 1992); and
- a single interview structure is usually employed to cover the three separate purposes of mutual preview, assessment, and negotiation.

These weaknesses come into sharper contrast as the types of interview in common use are described. Five main types can be identified:

- one-to-one interviews
- panel interviews
- series interviews
- stress interviews
- biographical interviews following the WASP model

One-to-one interviews

The solitary, one-to-one interview remains the mainstay of most organizations' selection procedures (Shackleton and Newell, 1991). This is the case despite the research findings reviewed in the previous chapter indicating that there is simply too much information for the interviewer to deal with in one single interaction. For this reason, interviewer skills are especially crucial in the one-to-one interview since the interviewer will be attempting to:

- *Interpret* the candidate's reply to the last question;
- *think* of their next question;
- *control* the interaction overall by following some preplanned questioning strategy; and ultimately to
- *form* an overall impression of suitability on the candidate.

Given these simultaneously occurring tasks, it is perhaps not surprising that interviewers are liable to make errors in their outcome decisions. One response to reduce information overload on the interviewer is the use of multiple interviewers acting as a panel.

Panel interviews

Panel interviews, involving anything from two to thirty interviewers, pose particular problems of coordination and control. Indeed, some of the most unprofessional interviewing practices the authors have come across have been where panel interviews are being conducted. This is unfortunate since adhering to four obvious conditions will resolve many of these problems of coordination:

- Decide in advance who is chairing the interview, and the chair's role;
- Agree the basic format for the interview so that individual interviewers know their question areas and the planned order of events;
- Allocate primary responsibility to one panel member for taking notes throughout the interview;
- Agree which panel member is to answer which type of question from the candidate.

Essentially, it should be agreed beforehand *who does what and when*. We come on in chapter 5 to consider in more detail the steps to setting up effective panel interviews.

Series interviews

Series interviewing is where a number of one-to-one or panel interviews are conducted in close succession to each other. The rationale is that this procedure can in some way 'wear down the candidate's defences'. This is a serious misconception as successive interviewers more often than not merely obtain more of the same information. The danger, of course, is that this process becomes a wasteful duplication of effort, rather than successive interviewers eliciting new information to add into the decision making process. Series interviews can be of real value, on the other hand, as long as each interviewer covers distinctly different aspects of the candidate's application.

Stress interviews

A more damaging sign of poor interviewing skills is the use of stress-type interviews. Here the interviewer sets up a stressful or difficult situation for the candidate to deal with and evaluates his or her response accordingly.

A striking example comes from one of the author's research experience into graduate selection and serves as an illustration of the abuse of interviewer power by stress interviewing (Anderson, 1988). The interviewer involved was recruiting pharmacy graduates to train as dispensing pharmacists in a chain of retail shops. His approach was to invite the candidate in and ask them to take a seat, followed by his opening question: 'Tell me, are you heterosexual or homosexual?'! When asked later about his reasons for this approach he replied to the effect that pharmacists needed to be capable of handling personal health matters over the sales counter in a professional and confidential manner! The interviewees spoken to by the author after their interviews held a somewhat different perception of this strategy and most indicated that they would willingly accept job offers made by other organizations in preference to an offer from this company.

A host of other gambits for stress interviews have been witnessed by the authors, all of which are ethically, morally, or even legally dubious. Moreover, the accuracy of stress interviews remains unproven. In the light of the negative impressions of the organization created among candidates, stress interviews deserve no part in organizational selection procedures.

Biographical interviews using the WASP model

Many interviewers are already conducting focused biographical interviews using the WASP model without realizing it. The acronym stands for:

- **W**elcome the candidate
- **A**cquire information from the candidate
- **S**upply information to the candidate
- **P**art the interaction and close the interview

Table 4.1 summarizes the contents of the interaction during each phase of the model.

Following the initial *welcome* and introductions, the interviewer moves into the main phase of the model – that of *acquiring* information from the candidate. Working biographically or chronologically through the candidate's application the interviewer commences with the interviewee's family background and moves through educational and career achievements to the job role currently held by the candidate. Future career aspirations may then be discussed and noted in relation to the vacancy being recruited for. *Supplying* the candidate with job content and job context information is the next phase of the WASP model. In this phase the interviewee will lead and direct the interaction as the interviewer will be responding to their queries. Finally, the interviewer needs to *part* or close the conversation. This is best accomplished by letting the candidate know when they can expect to receive notification of any decision, or details of the next stage of the organization's selection procedure. To conclude the WASP model, the interviewer fills out an assessment of the candidate and completes any other administrative arrangements arising from the interview. It is a safe bet that many interviewers will recognize this format as one which they have themselves used in conducting employment interviews.

Case example 4.1 sets out details from which a biographical interview role play may be developed. One suggestion is that groups work in sets of three – one person role playing the interviewer, one as interviewee, and one person acting as observer to the interview, making notes on the style and strategy of both participants. Groups can then debrief one another using the questions provided in the case example.

Table 4.1 The WASP model

Phase	Feature	Action
Welcome	Meeting and introductions	Handshakes. Thank candidate for coming. Introductions to other interviewers.
	Structuring	Explain to candidate the nature and structure of the interview.
Acquire	Family	Family background. Early life experiences.
	Education	Primary/secondary/higher/professional. Subjects chosen and why. Performance versus expectations. Positions of responsibility held.
	Career progression	Early posts through to current position. Duties performed. Liked and disliked duties. Examples of behaviour in different situations. Skills gained. Strengths and weaknesses. Relevance of current duties for post applied for.
	Career aspirations	Reason for current application. Short-, medium- and longer-term career aspirations. Desired job functions. Geographical mobility. Task preferences.
Supply	Job Content	Task responsibilities as per job description. Respond to candidate's questions and queries. Organizational expectations of job incumbent performance. Realistic career prospects.
	Job context	Terms and conditions of employment. Relocation provisions. Training and development procedures.
Part	Loose ends	Deal with any outstanding matters. Candidates' travelling expenses.
	Expectations	Explain next stage of selection procedure. Tell candidate when they should expect a decision.
	Close	Handshake. Thank candidate for attending.
	Assessment	Complete candidate assessment form. Action next phase of the selection procedure. Deal with administrative arrangements.

Case Example 4.1

Role play scenario: a biographical interview using the WASP model

Instructions   You are role-playing an interview for a clerical trainee position within Jupiter Stationery and Equipment PLC. You are given the following details:

- Company information
- Job advertisement
- Job description
- Candidate application form

Work in groups of three, with one person acting as interviewer, one as interviewee, and one as observer. Prepare and conduct a biographical interview using the WASP model for this vacancy.
   Approximate time limitations are as follows:

- Preparation time – 10 minutes
- Interview duration – 30 minutes
- Follow-up-questions – 10 minutes
- Total – 50 minutes

JUPITER STATIONERY AND EQUIPMENT PLC COMPANY INFORMATION

History

Established in 1947 as a manufacturer of foolscap files and other stationery items, the company expanded rapidly through the 1950s and won several large contracts, including the sole supplying of stationery to UK universities – a contract which to still holds.

Profitability

In every financial year since it inception, the company has made a trading profit. In 1993 turnover was £20 million, gross profit being £2.5 million. As the market leader, our position remains stable, and profitability looks encouraging.

Manufacturing

Ninety per cent of products are manufactured at the Birmingham head office plant, the remaining ten per cent being produced by the Bristol works.

Product range

We supply a wide range of stationery items (from box files to desk tidies, from paper clips to pencils, etc.) and an extensive office equipment range (e.g., filing cabinets and 'tailor made' executive desks). The total product range currently exceeds 200 separate items.

Personnel

We employ 600 staff in total: 530 at Birmingham, 70 at Bristol.

Board of directors

Chairman	R. B. Taylor, OBE
Managing	S. T. V. Jones
Production	V. Short
Marketing	T. A. Jefferson
Personnel	J. C. Clarke
Sales	C. T. Andrews
Financial	G. C. Coombes
Planning	D. D. Roberts
Secretary	J. B. A. Smythe

JOB ADVERTISEMENT JUPITER STATIONERY AND EQUIPMENT PLC CLERICAL TRAINEE – FIXED-TERM CONTRACT

As the market leader supplying stationery and office equipment worldwide, Jupiter has a vacancy for a graduate trainee based at our head office in Birmingham.

The successful candidate will complete our twelve-month inter-departmental training programme, which has been established since 1972 and incorporates intensive exposure to all the company's sections. Standards are unquestionably high, and the training is personally demanding in terms of expected commitment from the person appointed. Depending on performance, this one-year fixed-term contract may be renewed or transformed into a permanent contract.

In return we offer an excellent starting salary and comprehensive fringe benefits, including discount on company products.

SUMMARY JOB DESCRIPTION

1 Job Title

Name of job: Clerical trainee
Department: Personnel
Section: Training
Location: Birmingham head office

2 Job Summary – duties, operations and procedures involved, including degree of difficulty

Twelve-month inter-departmental training programme performing job functions in each department as detailed below:
Accounts: Credit controller
Production: Operator
Marketing: Publicity assistant
Sales: Trainee representative

3 Responsibility – areas of responsibility and job grading

Job function reports to the section supervisor in each department but, additionally, the personnel officer completes monthly reports on progress and makes recommendations as necessary.

4 Physical Nature

Varied, some physical work involved, but mostly light, clean and indoors.
Driving licence not essential for trainee representative post.

5 Social Nature

Varies according to department. Due to relatively short placements in each department (around three months) the trainee must be able to integrate quickly.

6 Training

Training for each job function conducted by section supervisor. Additionally, the trainee is required to attend a three-day induction course at Birmingham head office (unpaid) prior to commencement of the contract.

7 Conditions of Employment

Fixed-term contract: Twelve months duration. Salary negotiable.
37.5 hours per week, Monday-Friday, 9 am–1 pm, 2 pm–5 pm
20 days annual leave plus 8 statutory days
Pension contributions not applicable
Sickness scheme – SSP only
Car allowance – not applicable
Other benefits – 10% discount on company goods
                    Subsidized staff restaurant

APPLICATION FORM

Surname: *Brown*

Forenames: *Carol Jane*

Address: *15 Rotton Park Road*
        Edgbaston
        Birmingham
        B16 9JH

Telephone number: *021 413 71249*

Date of birth: *18 October 1963*

Place of birth: *Portland, Dorset, England*

Nationality: *British*

Single/married: *Single*

Have you had any serious operation, illness or injury? *No*

Do you hold a current driving licence? *YES*

State any language spoken and degree of fluency.
  French: 'O' Level

EDUCATION:

Secondary Schools Attended:
  North Walsham Girls High School   *Sept 1975–June 1978*
  Runton Hill Girls School   *Sept 1978–June 1982*
  Cambridge Tutorial College   *Sept 1982–June 1983*

Examinations:

Ordinary Level
Mathematics, English Language   *June 1979*
Additional Maths, Physics
Chemistry, Biology, French   *June 1982*
English Literature, Art

Advanced Level	*English*		B
	Mathematics, Pure and Applied	*June 1982*	D
	Physics		E
	Mathematics, Pure and Applied		B
	Physics	*January 1983*	C

Other qualifications
  IBM System 80 Word Processing Certificate   *July 1983*

Positions of responsibility held at school and university:
School prefect, editor of the school magazine, captain of the house hockey team, Lector i.e., senior pupil responsible for selection and delivery of lessons held at chapel.

EMPLOYMENT:

June 1983–June 1986	*Clerical assistant*	*Lloyds Bank PLC*
June 1986–October 1989	*Administrative assistant*	*National & Provincial Building Society*
October 1989– January 1993	*Clerk*	*Smith & Jones Ltd*
January 1993– to date	*Unemployed due to redundancy*	

INTERESTS:

I very much enjoy reading, especially the works of nineteenth century authors, for example Jane Austen and Thomas Hardy. I find it a very satisfying form of relaxation which is not only enjoyable for its own sake but is also intellectually stimulating. I believe a general exposure to, and an interest in, the arts i.e., fine art, music and literature, to be very important in broadening a person's viewpoint and awareness of the world around them. I also enjoy sports such as lacrosse, hockey and squash, although enthusiasm certainly outweighs ability in my case. Hockey and lacrosse require positive teamwork and awareness of one's role in relation to fellow team members. Squash, on the other hand, requires quick thinking and forethought, and players must rely on their own reactions. Other interests include socializing and entertaining, and long walks or rides in the country where one can appreciate the beauty of nature and forget frenetic city life.

Follow-up questions

1 How did you feel the interview went?
2 Did the interview follow the WASP model exactly, or was the pattern more varied?
3 How well did the interviewer in your group control and direct the interaction? Balance both positive and negative comments if possible.
4 Would the interviewer have offered the job to Carol Brown, and would Carol Brown have accepted?

Too much of a good thing?

The WASP model is orderly and easy to apply in both one-to-one and panel interviews. Its drawback is, of course, that the interviewer attempts to cover too much ground in a single interview. Returning to the three purposes of interviewing – mutual preview, assessment, and negotiation – it can be noted that the WASP model encompasses all three objectives. By attempting to meet all three aims simultaneously, it can be the case that interviewers fail to achieve any one objective satisfactorily. The solution – to conduct more than one interview – while undeniably more costly, can pay substantial dividends. Ideally, we would recommend that recruiters consider three key modifications to maximize the contribution of interviews to their selection system:

● Mutual preview, assessment, and negotiation interviews are conducted over time and are clearly distinguished from one another;

- A single interviewer conducts the mutual preview and negotiation interviews;
- A panel of interviewers or a different single interviewer conducts the highly structured assessment interview.

To summarize, then, recruiters presently using biographical interviews based on the WASP model are encouraged to re-examine the aims and objectives for interviewing candidates in the first place. It is a safe bet that the use of multiple interviews will allow the separation of these purposes and in the longer term prove a more cost-effective and valid way of reaching selection decisions.

Recent developments in structured interviewing techniques

Significant strides have been made by selection researchers and by specialist personnel consultancies in structured interviewing techniques over recent years (Dipboye, 1992). We cannot hope to cover in this section all the variants of structured interview methods presently in use by recruiters, but our aim here is to describe some of the more popular formats. Evidence from recent surveys of selection practices in organizations, suggests that only a minority of organizations are presently using highly structured techniques (Shackleton and Newell, 1991). So, it is appropriate for us to devote some space to these techniques with the aim of evaluating their potential contribution to candidate assessment.

The most popular of the types of structured interview have been developed from two original sources:

- Patterned Behaviour Description Interviews (PBDI)
- Situational interviews

Patterned Behaviour Description Interviews (PBDIs)

Originally based on research work by Dr Tom Janz, then at the University of Calgary, Alberta, Canada, the PBDI has been shown to have high predictive validity and reliability (Janz, Hellervik and Gilmore, 1986). The procedure for establishing PBDIs is quite complex, but procedes as follows.

Job analysis is undertaken to establish *critical incidents* of on-the-job behaviour. Critical incident job analysis is designed to elicit, as its name suggests, critical or crucial incidents of job behaviour which distinguish between effective and ineffective performance

Table 4.2   Examples of critical incidents in various jobs

Job	*Effective response*	*Ineffective response*
Administration clerk in banking	On receiving an application for a loan, to log the date of receipt, name of applicant and amount requested.	Failing to log the application on the day of its receipt, or failing to note all details correctly.
Computer-controlled lathe operator	Through frequent monitoring of the component load-bearing guage, to regulate pressure applied when the load readout falls below minimum requirements.	Omitting to monitor the guage at frequent intervals. Failure to regulate pressure when load falls below minimum requirements.
Management training consultant	To gain regular feedback by checking the understanding of course delegates and to modify speed of delivery of material.	Failure to request feedback or to perceive its relevance. Failure to modify speed of delivery in response to feedback.
University researcher	To identify and conduct statistical analyses of data appropriate to the design of the research study.	Failure to identify correct statistical analysis procedures. Misinterpretation of their results.

(Flanagan, 1954). Table 4.2 shows some examples of critical incidents for different types of job.

Once these critical incidents have been identified, a range of *performance dimensions* are formed as categories or critical types of behaviour underpinning effective job performance. Janz et al. (1986) argue that between five and ten performance dimensions are usually sufficient to establish the PBDI procedure for most job roles. Dimension descriptions are then checked with the job supervisor to validate their accuracy, before being used as the basis for developing detailed themes of questions for the interview itself. During the interview the interviewer makes careful notes on the candidate's responses, at all times attempting to establish past behaviour in situations similar to those identified as critical incidents. The interviewer also probes for the reasons why the candidate behaved in the manner described.

Many derivatives of the PBDI have appeared over recent years under a variety of titles, including behavioural event interviews, criterion referenced interviews, and so on. Essentially though, despite some differences in format or style, most are based on the original PBDI developed in Canada.

As we mentioned, the research evidence on the PBDI so far is very encouraging, with studies showing comparatively high levels of predictive validity and reliability.

Situational interviews

The situational interview takes, in many ways, a similar approach to that of the PBDI. It grew out of the work of Gary Latham (1989), another Canadian work psychologist, and, like the PBDI, it has proven to be a valid and reliable approach. The similarity between the two approaches lies in their use of critical incident job analysis to reveal crucial facets of on-the-job behaviour. In the case of the situational interview, however, the questions derived from this analysis are future-orientated, rather than focused on the past behaviour of the applicant as in the PBDI.

In the situational interview, the candidate is asked, 'What would you do in this situation?'. Backing up these questions addressing hypothetical situations, the interviewer rates the candidate's replies on rating scales based on behavioural descriptions of possible responses (termed *Behaviourally Anchored Rating Scales*, or BARS). Figure 4.3 illustrates typical questions and rating scales which may be used in a situational interview for a retail sales assistant.

Each interviewer's overall score can be calculated on completion of the interview, the aim, of course, being to compare candidates responses (what they say they will do) with their actual behaviour (what they actually do once in the job). As to whether candidates actually do behave as they say they will, the research evidence on this so far has been encouraging – the situational interview has been reported as having high predictive validity (Latham, 1989). One

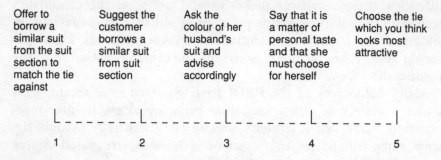

A female customer is choosing a silk tie to match her husband's best suit. Unsure of which to choose she asks your advice. What would be your response?

| Offer to borrow a similar suit from the suit section to match the tie against | Suggest the customer borrows a similar suit from suit section | Ask the colour of her husband's suit and advise accordingly | Say that it is a matter of personal taste and that she must choose for herself | Choose the tie which you think looks most attractive |

```
L _ _ _ _ _ _L _ _ _ _ _ _L _ _ _ _ _ _L _ _ _ _ _ _ _|
1              2              3              4              5
```

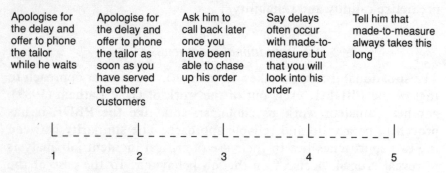

A particularly obstructive customer is complaining about the length of time he has been waiting for a made-to-measure suit. It is Saturday afternoon and a long queue of customers is waiting in line behind him. What would you do?

| Apologise for the delay and offer to phone the tailor while he waits | Apologise for the delay and offer to phone the tailor as soon as you have served the other customers | Ask him to call back later once you have been able to chase up his order | Say delays often occur with made-to-measure but that you will look into his order | Tell him that made-to-measure always takes this long |

```
L _ _ _ _ _L _ _ _ _ _ _ _ _ L _ _ _ _ L _ _ _ _ _ _|
1              2              3              4              5
```

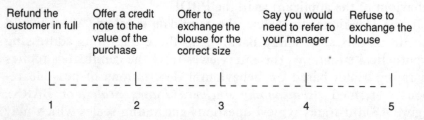

What would be your reaction if a customer returned a blouse bought three days earlier claiming that it did not fit?

| Refund the customer in full | Offer a credit note to the value of the purchase | Offer to exchange the blouse for the correct size | Say you would need to refer to your manager | Refuse to exchange the blouse |

```
L _ _ _ _ _ _L _ _ _ _ _ _ _L _ _ _ _ _ _L _ _ _ _ _ _|
1              2              3              4              5
```

Figure 4.3 Examples of situational interviewing scenarios for a retail sales assistant position.

doubt we should note, though, is the moderating effect of training on situational interview outcomes. In many types of job the candidate would expect to undergo thorough training before being required to respond to such scenarios – for example in the police service, social work, and in skilled operative job roles. It can therefore be a little unjust to expect the candidate to know appropriate responses prior to training, and this is certainly a limitation of situational interviews.

To summarize recent developments in structured interview techniques, HRM practitioners should note the benefits that these methods hold out for better interviewing practices and outcome decisions. The validity and reliability of techniques such as the PBDI and the situational interview are comparable to those attained by even the most accomplished selection techniques. Their accuracy depends entirely on setting up the structured interview properly and a final word of caution is therefore warranted. To construct these interview techniques properly one needs the support of specialist expertise.

Degrees of Structure: Some Conclusions

It is hoped that this chapter has stimulated some reflection on the part of the reader on degrees of structure for different types of interview. The structural continuum, ranging from totally unstructured, through focused, to highly structured, provides one way of considering the wide variety of types of interview being conducted today. The inescapable conclusion from this discussion of interview structures and formats is that there is no one best way to conduct a selection interview. 'It all depends' is the maxim which should serve as the guiding principle for matching interview function with an appropriate degree of structure. To restate the case, mutual preview interviews are most appropriately conducted as focused interviews, assessment interviews should be administered on a highly structured basis, using pre-formatted Behaviourally Anchored Rating Scales, and negotiation interviews conducted using a semi-unstructured design.

Summary Propositions

1   All interviews can be placed along a 'structural continuum' ranging from totally unstructured interviews, through focused interviews, to totally structured interviews.
2   The appropriate degree of structure depends on interview function and objectives.

3   One-to-one and panel interviews are both valuable in different circumstances, as are series interviews if properly planned.
4   Stress-type interviews are of negligible value in employee selection.
5   Different types of interview are most appropriately based on different degrees of structure:
    (a)   Mutual preview interviews using a focused structure;
    (b)   Assessment interviews using a highly structured approach; and
    (c)   Negotiation interviews using a semi-unstructured design.

Notes

1   See also P. Herriot (1987) The Selection Interview, in P. Warr (ed.) *Psychology at Work* (Harmondsworth: Penguin).

References

Anderson, N. R. (1988) *Interviewer Impression Formation & Decision Making in the Graduate Selection Interview: A Theoretical and Empirical Analysis*, Unpublished PhD Thesis, University of Aston, UK.

Dipboye, R. L. (1992) *Selection Interviews: Process Perspectives* (Cincinnati: South-Western Publishing Co.).

Eder, R. W. and Ferris, G. R. (eds) (1989) *The Employment Interview: Theory, Research, and Practice* (Newbury: Sage).

Flanagan, J. C. (1954) The Critical Incident Technique, *Psychological Bulletin*, 51, 327–58.

Janz, T., Hellervik, L. and Gilmore, D. C. (1986) *Behavior Description Interviewing: New, Accurate, Cost Effective* (Massachusetts: Allyn & Bacon).

Latham, G. P. (1989) The Validity, Reliability, and Practicality of the Situational Interview, in R. W. Eder, & G. R. Ferris, (eds), *The Employment Interview*. (Newbury: Sage).

Millar, R., Crute, V. and Hargie, O. (1992) *Professional Interviewing* (London Routledge).

Shackleton, V. J. and Newell, S. (1991) Management selection: a comparative survey of methods used in top British & French companies, *Journal of Occupational Psychology*, 64, 23–36.

Torrington, D. and Hall, L. (1987) *Personnel Management: A New Approach*, (London: Prentice-Hall IPM).

Part II

The Skills of Successful
Selection Interviewing

In this part of the book we focus upon the domain-relevant skills needed to conduct, and be the recipient of, successful selection interviews. Interviewing and being interviewed are dependent upon high-level cognitive and social skills, the appropriate enactment of which will determine interview outcomes from the perspective of both the interviewer and the candidate. Developing these themes into a cognitive-social skills approach to interview processes and decision making, chapters 5, 6 and 7 which comprise part II of this book, describe in detail the components of this approach.

5

Interview Skills I: Cognitive-Social Skills and Preparation

'Be prepared'
Scouting proverb

Setting the Scene

Up until this point in the book we have been concerned with some of the more formal aspects of interview design, the place of interviews in selection systems, their structure and format, and the picture provided by interview research. The intention in the three chapters forming part II is to focus more specifically upon the *skills* needed by the interviewer to perform successful selection interviews. In this chapter we consider the skills needed to set up effective interviews, especially those of *preparation* for the interview. In chapter 6 we describe the skills needed to actually *conduct* the interview in a manner which maximizes the chances of making accurate and fair outcome decisions, and in chapter 7 we review the *decision making* skills in practice.

A Cognitive-Social Skills Model of Interviewing

Regardless of the type or format of the interview, there is a core portfolio of skills necessary to conduct interviews in a professional manner. This may sound a rather far-reaching claim given the sheer diversity of types of interview we have outlined in the preceding chapters. It is important, however, to note that all selection interviews, at whatever stage in the selection process, and based upon

Table 5.1 Social and cognitive domain-relevant skills for conducting selection interviews

Social domain		Cognitive domain	
Rapport development	To set interviewees at ease and to establish good rapport with them to facilitate self-disclosure	Perceiving	To perceive or recognize the relevance of pieces of data emerging from the interaction
Empathic listening skills	To display empathic listening skills through appropriate verbal and non-verbal behaviour	Interpreting	To interpret emergent information correctly and to allocate individual data appropriate weightings reflecting their importance
Process management	To have an appreciation of, and be able to influence, the processual flow of social interaction during the interview	Integrating/ assimilating	To integrate multiple data (often from multiple sources, and sometimes conflicting in meaning) into an overall impression or profile of the candidate
Questioning strategies	To use appropriate questioning strategies to elicit accurate and comprehensive information from the candidate	Decision making	To compare candidate profiles with person and job specifications, with each other and with hiring quotas to arrive at outcome decisions
Note-taking	To make useful notes during the interview to remind the recruiter of key points and significant incidents		

Note
See chapter 3, figure 3.3, for an expanded description of cognitive skills.

whatever structural approach, share common elements in terms of both the *content* and *process* of the interaction. These include:

- To *obtain information* from the other party – preferably as accurate as one can secure given the other party's vested interest to fake-good (i.e., to portray information in as favourable a light as possible);
- To *give information* on oneself, or, for the recruiter, on one's organization;
- To *interpret information* given by the other – in the light of likely faking, for instance, by counter-referencing to other sources of data;
- To *progress the relationship forward* – the need here is for both parties to feel that they have made some headway as a result of the interview rather than just covering old ground once again. For instance, candidates having to endure a number of series interviews with each interviewer covering much the same question areas often express understandable dissatisfaction with the procedure as, from their perspective, progress is being hampered.

These four elements are present in all types of interview, with each element present to a greater or lesser extent. There is thus an underlying range of *skills*, essentially *cognitive* and *social* in nature, needed to conduct interviews successfully. Table 5.1 lays out these skills in overview, but we would emphasize that, in reality, the cognitive and social domains are inextricably bound together. For instance, to secure the data needed to commence forming impressions of the candidate, a largely cognitive skill, the interviewer has to have used appropriate social skills in the interaction to have elicited this information. These impressions may well then be the trigger for further social-domain skills, such as follow-up questions or checking of one's understanding.

Our intention is not to discuss in detail these domain-relevant skills here since much of this material is covered in the following two chapters. However, we should note the complexity of either cognitive or social-domain skills in isolation, let alone in the situation of the interview which demands simultaneous usage of both skill domains.

Preparing for the Interview: Some Ground Rules

We have previously noted that from the point of view of the candidate, the invitation to attend the organization's offices for interview will often be their one and only chance to see the organization 'from the inside' and to meet with its representative – the interviewer. As one author puts it '. . . The interviewer stands proxy for the organization as a whole' (Herriot, 1987, p. 152).

This onus of responsibility on the interviewer is therefore quite burdensome and includes the following key responsibilities:

- To *plan* the interview in advance based upon personal details already submitted by the applicant;
- To *take into account* the results of ability and personality tests in these plans, if they are available;
- To *elicit* relevant and comprehensive information from the candidate using appropriate social skills;
- To *interpret* this information correctly using cognitive information processing skills;
- To *provide* the candidate with job-relevant information;
- To be *conscious* that their own behaviour is being monitored by the interviewee.

It is therefore of paramount importance that every interview is adequately prepared for if the interviewer is to achieve his or her objectives. This is not just an empty plea from two academic authors writing a book on successful selection interviewing. The Institute of Personnel Management, in its most recent Code of Professional Conduct in Recruitment states categorically:

Recruiters must ensure that:
- the interviewers are fully conversant with the job specification and person specification applicable in the vacancy;
- questions are designed to obtain information for assessing against job related criteria, questions which could be construed as discriminatory are avoided and where information is requested for monitoring purposes, this has been made clear to the applicant;
- the approach to interview structure and content is applied consistently to all candidates interviewed for a specific vacancy;
- candidates are kept fully informed of changes in interview times and consideration is given to their time constraints;
- applicants are informed of the interview process, test procedures where applicable, the terms and conditions of employment, the time scale of the recruitment process and the appointment procedure; and
- all members of the organization with whom the interviewee may come into contact are fully aware of recruitment procedures and policies. (Institute of Personnel Management, 1991, page 7)

To set some ground rules for effective interview preparation interviewers need to consider five main areas:

1 Location and set-up
2 General documentation
3 Format, structure, and rating procedures
4 Question generation and hypothesis formulation
5 Closing-down and following-up

Location and set-up

Many of the existing 'how to interview' guidebooks delve into the intricate details of laying out the room for interview, the positioning of chairs, arrangements at reception, and so on. There is no one 'best way' of organizing such logistics, but it is worth remembering a few key points:

- *Appropriate formality* – the interviewee will probably be expecting a reasonably formal set up. Excessive informality may result in an increase in their anxiety rather than the intended decrease!
- *Comfort* – the layout and furnishings should be sufficiently comfortable to tolerate for fairly long periods of time. Plush, upholstered reclining chairs may be somewhat excessive! Remember, the candidate may take an image of the layout away and assume it represents the organization and its culture.
- *Tranquility* – distractions should be avoided at all costs and so the interview room needs to be protected from unwanted interruptions either in the form of phone calls or personal interruptions. A trade-off needs to be made here against totally isolating and separating the room which may leave candidates with a biased perception of the organization.
- *Practicality* – One of the authors was once interviewed by a panel of interviewers so large in number that an elongated table had to be erected to seat all of them. The furthest interviewer was some 8 metres away from the candidate and a seating plan had been placed on the table in front of the candidate to let it be known who sat where!
  The practicality of the situation is that the layout needs to facilitate social interaction and so particular care needs to be taken with panel interviews.
- *Efficiency and courtesy* – Dealing with the candidate in an efficient but courteous manner in all aspects of communication with them throughout the selection process (e.g., written communications, interview, etc.) will make the most favourable impression of the organization. It will also attract the best candidates to accept any offer of employment.

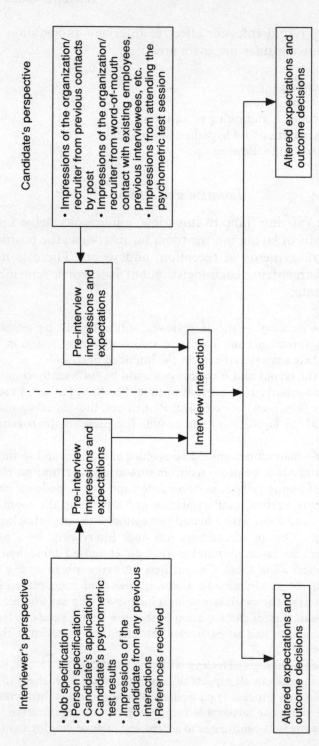

Figure 5.1 A model of the impact of documentary information and other prior sources upon interview processes.

Candidate's perspective

- Impressions of the organization/recruiter from previous contacts by post
- Impressions of the organization/recruiter from word-of-mouth contact with existing employees, previous interviewees, etc.
- Impressions from attending the psychometric test session

Pre-interview impressions and expectations

Interview interaction

Altered expectations and outcome decisions

Interviewer's perspective

- Job specification
- Person specification
- Candidate's application
- Candidate's psychometric test results
- Impressions of the candidate from any previous interactions
- References received

Pre-interview impressions and expectations

Altered expectations and outcome decisions

General documentation

In most instances, the interview process will be driven by documentary information already in the possession of the recruiter. The application form probably serves as the most significant 'driver', but other sources of data also need to be taken into account, including the job and person specifications, references received prior to interview, and the results of psychometric tests.[1] Figure 5.1 illustrates this point from the perspective of both the interviewer and the candidate, arguing that multiple sources of data combine to create pre-interview impressions and expectations which significantly impinge upon interview processes and outcomes.[2] It is consequently most important for the interviewer to ensure that all sources of documentary information on the candidate are in their possession prior to the interview, and that these data have been interpreted and weighted accurately and appropriately. This may appear an axiomatic recommendation, but all too often interviewers do their best to 'muddle through' with only incomplete documentary information in their possession due to administrative inefficiency. We consider this process in some detail later in this chapter.

Format, structure and rating procedures

The third area of effective preparation prior to the interview concerns making the format, structure, and candidate rating procedures known to the interviewer(s) in advance. This is particularly true in the case of panel interviews, where members of the panel can be drawn from a variety of departmental backgrounds, where, in some cases, the format of the interview procedure will not be understood by all interviewers. This attention to the ensuing procedure of the interview is, of course, a matter largely of common sense. But it is advisable at least to check the intended interview format and structure, as well as to refresh one's memory and understanding of the candidate assessment form prior to the interview.

By taking these relatively simple precautionary steps it is likely that the interview process will be:

● More orderly and professional from the candidate's point of view;
● More accurate and comprehensive in collecting and collating information from the candidate;

- More valid, due to the interviewers directing their attention to specific aspects of candidate behaviour required of them in the assessment and rating procedure.

This is not the stage at which the interviewer should be attempting to actually set up interview format, structure, or rating procedures. This should clearly have been done well in advance of the interview, as we argued in chapter 4. Thus, the sight of the interviewer hurriedly trying to establish these matters is a sign of poor preparation – the aim at this stage is simply to remind oneself of these procedures so that the interview runs as smoothly as possible.

Question generation and hypothesis formulation

We face some difficulties in illustrating the dynamic real-life processes of question generation and hypothesis formulation from documentary source data through the medium of the printed page. Recruiters each have their own idiosyncratic methods of doing this. Data will often be received at different times, possibly over several weeks, and information will be interpreted differently for different types of job. On the other hand, the cognitive processes of converting documentary information into question areas are universal. They include some of the cognitive skills noted earlier in this chapter, but others besides. These include the skill to:

- *Recognize* the potential importance of data either included or omitted from all sources available;
- *Note* this piece of information or its omission;
- *Formulate* alternative explanations or hypotheses to be followed-up, carefully avoiding any actual *decision making* at this premature stage;
- *Generate* questions to probe into these hypotheses, giving due regard to the rights of the applicant and ethical constraints on personal questions;
- *Generate* more extensive question areas to follow-up other issues and aspects not fully covered by existing documentary data.

To illustrate these skills in practice, case example 5.1 presents documentary details on a candidate applying for the post of management accountant, a senior managerial position in the given organization. It shows how the authors have worked through this fictitious application, noting areas for further questioning at interview and possible hypotheses to explain specific issues of concern. The case may be used, however, without referring to our workings. This allows the reader to construct their own question areas and hypotheses, and then to compare these with our areas of questioning. Our workings are comprehensive and extensive, and it would be unusual for the recruiter in real-life to make notes in such detail as in most circumstances just a short note under each heading will suffice (Courtis, 1988). The case example does, nevertheless, illustrate how question areas and hypothetical explanations can be generated from applicaation details, and the extent to which this process can be taken if desired.

Case Example 5.1

*Generating questions and hypothetical explanations from
the application form*

SUMMARY JOB DESCRIPTION:

Post:	Management accountant
Grade:	Senior Managerial Grade I
Salary:	Up to £30,000 p.a. starting
Department:	Management Accounts, Leicester head office
Reports to:	Director of Finance
Responsible for:	Staff of 23 (at current headcount) in Financial Accounts and Management Accounts Sections.
Summary responsibilities:	(1) To be personally responsible for all aspects of the organization's management accounting system.
	(2) To be personally responsible for some aspects of the organization's financial accounting systems, including financial reports to the board of directors.
	(3) To take responsibility for staff in the Management Accounts Department, including all aspects of their performance review and training needs analysis.

SUMMARY PERSON SPECIFICATION:

Professional qualifications:	Full membership of an appropriate professional accountancy body, e.g. Association of Cost and Management Accountants (ACMA), or Association of Chartered Accountants (ACA).
Academic qualifications:	To degree level or equivalent.
Managerial experience:	A minimum of 10 years relevant managerial experience covering both financial and management accounts functions. Evidence of in-depth and comprehensive understanding of current cost accounting practices. Directly comparable experience may have been gained in an equivalent role in a smaller company, or as a 'number 2' in an equivalent sized accounts department.
Personal qualities:	Must command respect and trust. Approachability is important, as is loyalty to the company. High levels of commitment and motivation are essential as the post-holder will be required to work long hours and occasional weekends.

APPLICATION FORM:

Name:	Richard George Westwood
Address:	13 The Copt Manor Heath London SW19 4BZ
Date of birth:	1.7.60
Personal status:	Married
Children:	Three (ages 7, 3, and 8 months)
Secondary education:	Queensbury Grammar School Crookes Sheffield

	1976: 8 Ordinary level (Maths, English, Geography, French, German, Computer Studies, English Literature)
	1978: 4 Advanced level (Maths 'A', English Literature 'C', German 'C', French 'D')

University education: October 1979–June 1983: BSc in
Modern Languages and Management,
University of Nottingham
2 (ii) honours degree
Third year of course spent in Lille,
France (6 months), and Cologne,
Germany (6 months) in placement jobs:

France: Language assistant
Lille University
Department of English
Studies

Germany: Accounts assistant
BAT Industries (Europe)
Ltd
Cologne Head Office
Cologne, North Germany

Final year project completed in
reviewing the differences and
similarities between company
accounting procedures across the EC,
with particular reference to asset
discounting and depreciation
provisions

Professional education: 1984–1990:   ACMA Professional
Examinations Fully
qualified June 1990

CAREER HISTORY:

Dates	Position	Employer	Key responsibilities	Leaving salary
July 1977– Sept. 1979	Management trainee	ABC Ltd Harrow Vale	Training placements in a variety of departments	£5,600
August 1983– Jan. 1986	Senior accounts clerk	XYZ Industries, Glasgow office	Provision of financial accounts to senior management accountant	£12,400

Dates	Position	Employer	Key responsibilities	Leaving salary
Jan. 1986–July 1990	Assistant management accountant	XYZ Industries, UK head office	Range of management and financial accounting duties; supervising section of 4 staff	£17,200
July 1990–to date	Management accountant	"	Personal responsibility for all aspects of management accounts, final year accounts production, and budgeting reports to the Board of Directors. Managing a staff of 14 in financial and management accounts sections	£24,500 (current salary)

Closing-down and following-up

The fifth and final area of preparation prior to the interview is really one of ensuring that all necessary steps have been taken for the interview to run smoothly and, hopefully, for accurate decisions to be made as a result. Figure 5.2 provides a 20-item checklist covering these points and is designed as an *aide memoire* for recruiters at this stage.

At this stage of preparation for the interview the only outstanding issues concern follow-up correspondence with the candidate after the interview. In other words, has it been agreed what the next stage of the selection procedure will be and how the candidate is to be informed of any decision reached following the interview? It is good practice in the closing stages of the interview to structure the candidate's expectations of what is to follow. It is consequently advisable for the interviewer or interviewers to have agreed this in advance and to have decided how this will be communicated to the candidate.

Concluding Comments

In this chapter we have been concerned to highlight the importance of careful preparation as a necessary antecedent to successful selection interviews. Interview preparations can often go astray through a combination of administrative inefficiency and a lack of control

Checklist of points of preparation for the interview		
Documentary information on the candidate	YES	NO
1 Have all sources of information on the candidate been received and collated?		
– Application form	☐	☐
– CV	☐	☐
– Test results	☐	☐
– Medical	☐	☐
– Others	☐	☐
2 Have the job description and person specification been scrutinized and understood thoroughly by the interviewer(s)?	☐	☐
3 Have references been received if these have been requested in advance?	☐	☐
4 Has the application been scrutinized to generate question areas and hypothetical explanations?	☐	☐
5 Have particularly important issues for questioning at interview been noted?	☐	☐
Correspondence with the candidate	YES	NO
6 Has the candidate been sent full details of the interview location, date, and time?	☐	☐
7 Has the candidate been provided with a Realistic Job Preview? (See chapter 2)	☐	☐
8 Has the candidate been informed of the purpose of the interview? (If not, some introductory comments by the interviewer(s) are called for.)	☐	☐
Location and venue	YES	NO
9 Has the interview room been properly set up?	☐	☐
10 Has the receptionist been informed of the applicant's attendance for interview?	☐	☐
11 Have all sources of interruption been eliminated? (Transfer of phones, indicating the room is engaged, etc.)	☐	☐
Preparation for the interview process	YES	NO
12 Has the structure and format of the interview been decided upon? (See chapter 4)	☐	☐
13 If a panel interview is being conducted, has it been agreed which members of the panel will cover different aspects of the application?	☐	☐
14 Has it been decided how to handle unforeseen areas of questioning which arise during the interview?	☐	☐
15 Has it been agreed how to anwer the candidate's queries and how best to provide them with information on the organization and the job role applied for?	☐	☐
Decision making procedure and follow-up	YES	NO
16 Has the decision making process been agreed upon?	☐	☐
17 Is the candidate assessment form agreed upon and known to the interviewer(s) in advance?	☐	☐
18 Are the weights allocated to each rating dimension agreed and known in advance? (See also chapter 4)	☐	☐
19 Has it been decided how to close the interview and how to structure the candidate's expectations on what happens next?	☐	☐
20 Have all follow-up procedures for correspondence with the candidate been decided upon and set up within the organization?	☐	☐

Figure 5.2   Checklist of points of preparation for the interview.

Table 5.2 Question generation and hypothesis formulation profile

Name: Richard Westwood
Post: Management accountant (SMI)

	Area of query	Overarching question	Follow-up questions	Hypothetical explanations	Comments and reminders for interviewer
1	Education	Given his grade 'A' at A-Level in Maths, why did he choose to do modern languages and management at university?	Is figure work his real area of competence, but languages his area of personal interest? Is this why he is now applying – to combine his accountancy skills with his German language ability?	Career opportunities in accountancy are better than in languages. Financial rewards are significantly better in accountancy. An attempt to merge two strands of his career. Continuing and unresolved uncertainty between choice of two career paths.	How important is fluent German to job performance?
2	Placement year	What exactly did he do at XYZ Industries, Cologne?	Was this relevant accounting experience or just a clerical assistant placement? The German accent around Cologne is particularly heavy, can he understand the accent around Munich?	Just took what he could get – real motivation to do accountancy work? Can speak textbook German and understand the Cologne dialect only.	Query over whether his career plan was consciously thought through.
3	Professional education	Why choose ACMA not ACA, or one of the others?	What particularly appealed in ACMA? Again, was this opportunistic, or intentionally strived for? Why did it take him 6 years to complete ACMA?	Wanted an 'industrial' accountancy training. Merely took the best on offer. Was coerced into this by employer. Failed one year.	Motivation query – did he drift into ACMA or purposely choose to do it?

4	Career history	Can he give much greater depth of information on ● job responsibilities ● reasons for moving on in each job? ● behaviour in key situations in each job? Can he describe his present job in terms of ● accountancy responsibilities ● staff supervision?	How did his career develop in the way that it has? Can he describe his behaviour in situations similar to ones he may have to face as the Management Accountant? How comparable is his present job with this vacancy? Why has he applied for this job – he has been quite successful within XYZ Industries?	Opportunistic – did not plan out his career in any detail. No hypothesis formed. Considerable comparability. Career prospects and promotion opportunity.	See above. Be wary of candidate faking on this query – check comparability by written reference request.
5	Others	How willing is he and his family to relocate to Leicester? Is he prepared to spend considerable time away from home, including working some evenings and weekends?	Has he discussed this prospect with his family? What are their feelings? Same line of questioning as above.	No hypothese formed. Does not realise the true extent of this.	NB: our relocation package is poor compared to other employers. Be conscious of this possible area of difficulty. Provide RJP information on this point.

mechanisms in the selection procedure to draw the attention of the recruiter to incomplete aspects in their preparation. Especially under the fire-fighting pressures experienced by recruiters in periods of intensive selection, it is easy to overlook some areas of preparation for forthcoming interviews. Our advice, then, is to guard against this in two ways:

● Be conscious of the importance of preparing fully for every interview;
● Institute checking procedures, such as the 20-item checklist suggested in figure 5.2, designed to ensure that all aspects of pre-interview preparation have been carried out.

Summary Propositions

1 Successful selection interviewers possess highly developed cognitive and social skills which they bring to bear on the interview situation in order to *elicit* and *interpret* comprehensive information from the candidate.
2 Effective preparation prior to the interview is of paramount importance for successful selection decisions.
3 Effective preparation demands attention to five key areas:
   (a) location and set up;
   (b) documentation;
   (c) format, structure, and rating procedures;
   (d) question generation and hypothesis formulation;
   (e) closing-down and following-up.
4 Aspects of preparation are easily overlooked and the recruiter therefore needs to consciously guard against this tendency.

Notes

1 See, for instance, our suggestions for further reading in appendix I.
2 See also, N. Schmitt and B. W. Coyle, (1976) Applicant Decisions in the Employment Interview, *Journal of Applied Psychology*, 61, 184–92.

References

Courtis, J. (1988) *Interviews: Skills & Strategy* (London: IPM).
Herriot, P. (1987) The Selection Interview, in P. Warr, (ed) *Psychology at Work* (Harmondsworth: Penguin).
Institute of Personnel Management (1991) *The IPM Recruitment Code* (London).

6
Interviews Skills II: Social Skills at Interview

'... most interviewers seem to believe that their main means of acquiring information is to ask questions. There are, however, many ways of responding in order to encourage the interviewee to give information such as responding approvingly to what has been said, pausing briefly after the interviewee has spoken, paraphrasing the interviewee's comments or indeed giving an opinion on an issue and inviting a response.'

Millar, Crute and Hargie, *Professional Interviewing*, 1992

Aims of the Social Skills Perspective

In this chapter we aim to explore the portfolio of social skills needed to perform, and be the recipient of, successful selection interviews. Our intention is to describe these social skills in practice and to illustrate their applicability to different stages of the interview process by providing examples of each skill as a social interactional technique. As our quote by Rob Millar, Valerie Crute, and Owen Hargie at the head of this page hints, these skills extend far beyond merely asking questions of the candidate, to embrace a diverse range of techniques of which a variety of questioning strategies is only one component.

There are two parts to this chapter. First, we consider these skills from the perspective of the interviewer, then from the viewpoint of the candidate.

Interviewer Social Skills

Successful selection interviewers possess and apply a range of interpersonal social skills in order to elicit accurate and comprehensive information from candidates. In our cognitive-social model of interview skills outlined in chapter 5 (see figure 5.1), we defined six crucial areas of social skills for the interviewer:

- *Rapport development* – establishing an effective rapport with the candidate at the opening stages of the interview;
- *Empathic listening* – the verbal and non-verbal skills of attentive, empathic listening;
- *Process management* – managing the interaction successfully, including 'pacing' the communication flow and 'funnelling' from one topic to another;
- *Questioning strategies* – the use of different types of questions, including open, closed, probing, behavioural description, situational-type questions, and summarising/checking understanding;
- *Note-taking* – taking notes during the interview without appearing to be making copious personal comments on the candidate;
- *Closing-down* – bringing the interaction to an acceptable close while giving the interviewee a chance to ask any remaining questions and imparting some idea of the next stage in the selection process.

Let us consider each in turn.

Rapport development

In the early stages of the interview the aim of the interviewer is twofold:

- To set the candidate at ease so they may do themself justice in the interaction;
- To establish rapport with the candidate so as to facilitate self-disclosure and an uninhibited exchange of views.

These are both important objectives and, as the interview research has shown (see chapter 3), the initial stages of the interaction are by far the most important in influencing outcome decisions. Since these opening few minutes will go a long way toward establishing the tenor of the whole interview, care needs to be taken by the recruiter to develop an 'operational rapport' (Argyle, 1983) with the candidate. By this we mean that the interviewer needs to communicate a feeling of openness and trust to the candidate – in effect to allow the interviewee to *perceive* that the situation is non-threatening and that the interviewer is concerned to permit them a fair hearing of their strengths and weaknesses in relation to the job vacancy.

How can this best be achieved? The interviewer has two main channels of interpersonal communication at their disposal:

- *Verbal* – what they actually say;
- *Non-verbal* – or 'body language', how they say what they say.

Verbal communication (i.e., statements made) at this stage of rapport development need to be carefully handled by the interviewer, but could include one of several opening gambits:

Social pleasantries   For example:

'I hope you managed to find the building without too much trouble?'

'Thanks for taking the trouble to come in and talk with me. Do you have any restriction upon your time this afternoon?'

'Did you have far to travel this morning to find us? . . . You came over from Reading, didn't you?'

Setting the scene   For example:

'What I propose to do is to spend about thirty minutes working through your application, and then taking some time to answer any question you might have. Is that O.K.?'

'This is the first stage interview in our selection process, After talking with me I will pass you over to David Brown, our production manager, who will want to talk with you on the more technical side of you expertise. Is this O.K. as far as you are concerned?'

Progress report   For example:

'Let me tell you about the selection process for this vacancy to bring you up-to-date on progress so far. We advertised last month and from the forty applications received we have invited in six candidates for interview. You are one of those six.'

'So you replied to our advert placed in the Job Centre? Well, I have had three other people contact me. You are the first to be interviewed.'

All three strategies share the common characteristics of being *non-threatening* to the candidate and of encouraging their *participation*

Table 6.1 Non-verbal and verbal cues of empathic listening

	Non-verbal		Verbal
• Gaze	looking at the candidate for most of the time, particularly when they are speaking	• Minimal reinforcers	using para-linguistic verbal reinforcers to signal agreement for the other to continue speaking, e.g. 'uh, uh', 'mm . . .'
• Eye contact	meeting the candidate's glance to hold eye contact for a socially acceptable duration	• Interventive reinforcers	short reinforcement utterances to signal continuation (e.g. 'yes', 'I see', 'I understand')
• Orientation	facing the candidate almost square-on	• Minimal statements/ questions	reflection checking understanding summarizing
• Posture	maintaining an open posture to indicate accessibility	• Interventive statements/ questions	probing behavioural description questions situational questions
• Recline	slight forward lean to indicate interest and involvement		
• Facial expression	frequent use of positive facial expressions, including smiling		
• Head nods	Frequent use of nods of the head as a reinforcer		

in the process, for instance, by requesting their permission to follow a particular course of action. The aim is to allow the candidate to 'find their feet' in these early stages, before moving on to more probing and challenging lines of questioning later in the interview.

Non-verbal strategies of rapport development, usually referred to in the popular literature as body language (Argyle, 1983; Morris et al., 1979), overlap considerably with the skills of *empathic listening* which we describe below.

Empathic listening

Empathy – The power of projecting one's personality into, and so fully understanding, the object of contemplation (Shorter Oxford English Dictionary, Third Edition)

Conveying the impression of attentive, empathic listening to the interviewee is an important aspect of skilled interviewer perform-ance at all stages of the interaction, but particularly in the opening few minutes of the interview. Michael Argyle (1983) refers to this area of social skills as the 'signalling of attentiveness' to the other party. Several non-verbal and verbal cues can be used to achieve this, as illustrated in table 6.1.

It is the way in which these verbal and non-verbal behaviours are *combined* which conveys the most potent message of attentive listening. For instance, an open posture orientated directly toward the candidate with high levels of eye contact and frequent head nods, reinforced with timely minimal verbal reinforcers, such as 'uh, uh' will portray a generally pleasant and attentive impression to the candidate. One danger, though, is for the interviewer to attempt to mimic these behavioural cues, thus appearing to the candidate as *needing to try* to exhibit such positive reinforcers. Such behaviours can come across as being wholly false and unconvincing, and so interviewers need to develop their own particular style of empathic listening early in their careers which can then be developed over time with the benefit of interviewing experience.

Process management

The interview situation presents the recruiter with real problems of coordination and control, as many practising recruiters and HRM specialists will readily confirm. We mentioned in chapters 3 and 4

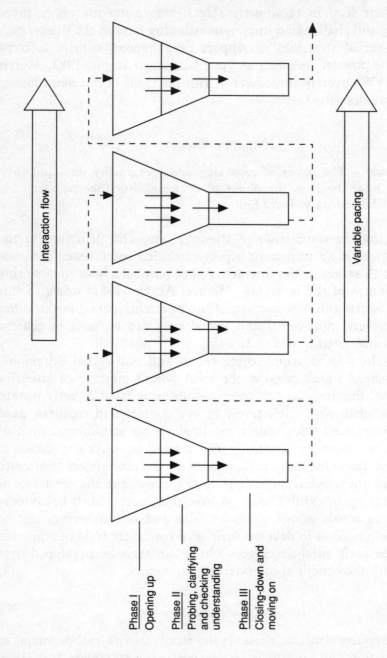

Interaction flow

Variable pacing

Phase I
Opening up

Phase II
Probing, clarifying
and checking
understanding

Phase III
Closing-down and
moving on

Figure 6.1 The process management skills of 'funnelling' and 'pacing'.

the difficulties inherent in attempting to manage the social interaction component of the interview while trying simultaneously to interpret and assimilate information given by the candidate. It is therefore vital for the interviewer to have a mastery of the main techniques of process management so as to avoid the interview deteriorating into a disorderly, informal conversation, guided by the candidate into areas which they know to be their real strengths (Kahn and Cannell, 1960), or guided by the interview into easy areas of questioning (e.g., hobbies) which may not be relevant.

The interviewer has two main strategies for managing the interview process – *funnelling* and *pacing*.

1   *Funnelling*   The strategy of funnelling through a number of different topics during the interview rally comprises six distinct sub-skills:

- *Sub-divide* the interview into an appropriate number of topics for conversation;
- *Open up* each topic using skillful questioning techniques;
- *Probe* into each topic so as to elicit further information from the candidate on points of particular concern;
- *Summarize* and check understanding resulting from probing questions;
- *Close-down* each topic once it has been exhausted as a seam of relevant data for selection decision making;
- *Move on* to the next topic of conversation by using appropriate social skills to indicate to the candidate that this is the intention of the interviewer.

Figure 6.1 illustrates graphically this process management technique. it shows that the overriding strategic intention is to control and coordinate the flow of interaction by *sub-dividing* the interview in advance into manageable topics or themes of enquiry. The total number of topics for questioning will vary from interview to interview, depending upon the depth and width of experience of the interviewee, lines of questioning generated by psychometric test results or work sample tests, and the type of interview being conducted (i.e., mutual preview, assessment, or negotiation). This process management strategy is therefore general to all types of interview in that it offers a model to guide the recruiter's interview plan. For instance in case example 5.1, described in chapter 5, it is likely that the interviewer preparing their plan to interview this candidate would incorporate five main themes or topics of enquiry – funnelling through from educational achievements to the candidate's placement year, to professional education, to career history, and finally to other areas of concern.

The technique of funnelling has the second advantage of highlighting the different types of social skills and questioning techniques needed by the interviewer at different stages of the interview.[1] Early on the interviewer needs the skills to *open up* a theme for conversation and, in so doing, to orientate the concentration of the interviewee toward this topic. Once the topic is established, the skilled interviewer is able to *probe* into specific aspects of the candidate's application arising in conversation with them. When the interviewer begins to feel that little new is emerging, then the skill is to perceive this 'point of diminishing returns'. That is, the point at which spending more time on this theme is dysfunctional since the information returns are getting progressively lower in comparison with moving on to a fresh topic for funnelling. Here, the interviewer needs to *summarize* progress so far and move the candidate on to the next area for probing questions. The third and final phase, then, is *closing-down* the theme and *moving on* to a new line of enquiry. Again, this demands social skills which are distinct from those needed to open up or to probe. The specific social and questioning skills that the interviewer needs to deploy at each of these three stages of funnelling are described in the following section of this chapter (Farr, 1982).[2]

2   *Pacing*   Pacing the interaction is the second prerequisite of process management for successful interviewing. This entails having a feel for the correct pacing of the interaction overall, but also being able to pace each stage of each topic in an appropriate manner. The skilful interviewer will pace each phase of the topic under discussion broadly as follows:

- *Opening up* – A gentle introduction to the topic, taking time to ensure that the interviewee understands precisely the area the interviewer wishes of discuss. Allow time for the candidate to re-orientate their thoughts to this topic, especially if it relates to their distant past history, such as school life or family background.
- *Probing* – Pacing at this stage is more a 'parry and thrust' activity of sharp moves forward to probe into areas of concern, interspersed with the interviewer checking their understanding and thus slowing down the pace of the interaction to rationalize progress made so far.
- *Closing-down and moving on* – The skilful interviewer will appear not to be actually doing this. The closure of one topic area needs to appear a

natural progression of the conversation since there is little else to be said on this theme. The skill is to move the interviewee on swiftly to the next topic, so starting over the funnelling cycle once again.

To really gain an appreciation of these techniques these is no better way than to practise them in the context of a recruitment scenario. Case example 6.1 provides just that – the scenario is to utilize your own curriculum vitae and to select a relevant job to which you would consider applying at this point in your career. This scenario can take up to sixty minutes to complete, but can be curtailed if that amount of time is not available.

Case Example 6.1

A role-play exercise to practise funnelling, pacing and empathic listening as process management strategies

Instructions Work in pairs. Spend some time reading through the other person's current curriculum vitae. Nominate a suitable job for this exercise. Use the techniques of question generation and hypothesis formulation (see chapter 5 for details) to plan a 15-minute interview with your partner. When planning the interview, consider carefully the themes or topics you wish to funnel through in the interview. Plan opening up, probing, and closing-down questions and statements for each topic. Consider also how you will pace the interaction at different stages, giving ample time to concentrate upon key issues arising from your partner's curriculum vitae. Take it in turns to acts as interviewer and candidate for your chosen job vacancy.

Questions/tasks

1 Give your partner constructive feedback on how well they managed the process as interviewer. Consider funnelling, skills, pacing skills and empathic listening skills, particularly their non-verbal behaviour as interviewer.
2 Did your interviewer partner appear relaxed in their task? Did they create the impression of needing further practice in these areas of social skills?
3 Where could your partner have improved their performance? Do any significant incidents stick out in your mind as key turning points?
4 Did your partner use a skilful style of empathic listening to encourage you to talk freely?

5 How well did your partner perform when role-playing as the candidate? Try to give constructive feedback on specific issues which arise during the interview.

Note This case example can also be used in two other ways:

- to practise in detail the skills of question generation and hypothesis formulation described in chapter 5;
- to practise the range of interview questioning strategies covered later in this chapter.

Approximate timings for this case example are as follows:

● Reading your partner's CV, generating questions, and formulating hypotheses		10 minutes
● Conducting each interview	– Interview A	15 minutes
	– Interview B	15 minutes
● Feedback to your partner	– First	10 minutes
	– Second	10 minutes
	Total	60 minutes

Questioning strategies

The fourth component of our social skills model of successful selection interviewing is that of interviewer questioning strategies. Interviews exist to allow the exchange of information between applicants and organizations. From the perspective of the interviewer it is unthinkable to propound a social skills model of interviewing which omits the range of questioning strategies at their disposal to elicit information from the candidate. Practising interviewers rarely pay conscious attention to their own style of questioning, as their focus is on making accurate selection decisions. Standing back from these pressures for a moment, it is possible to identify several highly useful questioning strategies, and several styles which are best avoided.

Useful techniques can be summarized as follows:

- open questions
- probing questions
- reflection
- checking/summarizing understanding

- behaviour description – type (BD) questions
- situational – type questions

Inadvisable techniques include:

- closed questions
- leading questions
- dysfunctional sidetracking
- personally intrusive questions
- discriminatory questions

Both strategies are described over the next few pages.

Useful Questioning Techniques

Open questions

The open question is the most valuable of all questioning techniques available to the recruitment interviewer. Used to get the interviewee talking freely about a topic area, it is an essential component of successful selection interviewing. It can take several forms, for example:

'I notice from your application that you are currently working as an insurance sales consultant for Y Corporation. *Tell me about your responsibilities.*'

'According to your CV, this is your third job since leaving university two years ago. *Describe to me your reasons for changing.*'

'You said a few minutes ago that your preference is for working outdoors. *What makes you say this?*'

'*Can you tell me* something about your reasons for applying for this vacancy?'

The open question is a potent means of information elicitation. If combined with the techniques of probing and reflection it becomes even more salient.

Probing questions

Used to follow up information from the candidate's application or data emerging from open questions during the interview itself, the probing question often takes the form of 'Why was it the case that . . .' For instance:

'In your CV you say that you took voluntary redundancy just over six months ago. *Why did you choose this course of action then?*'

'When we were talking a few minutes ago about your time at university, you said you specialized in Human Resource Management options on your MBA. *Why was this?*'

Reflection

Reflection as a technique is simply where the interviewer reflects or re-states the main thrust of the interviewee's previous statement. For example:

Example A

Candidate: 'I was working with JH plc, but wanted more excitement. So I become a broker working on the government bonds and futures trading floor of the stock exchange. I also felt it would offer better career prospects and rewards.'

Interviewer: 'So you felt that being a broker would be both a career jump and better paid, as well as being more exciting?'

Example B

On a training course on interviewing skills organized by one of the authors, one delegate enquired:

Delegate: 'I have heard a lot about this one technique – I think it's called reflection – but I don't know what it means exactly. Can you tell us about it?'

Author: 'So, you've heard about reflection but you're not quite sure what it entails and you would like me to spend a few minutes on it . . . ?

Delegate: 'If you could. I have heard that it . . .'

Another
delegate: 'He has just demonstrated it!'

Reflection involves re-stating, or paraphrasing, the other person's statement with the objective of reflecting it back to them, without further comment, for them to elucidate upon. Useful as a method for obtaining further information on a particular topic, reflection is particularly valuable as a minimal intervention technique used to follow up open or probing questions.

Summarizing/checking understanding

Open questions, probing questions, and reflection are all valuable methods in the repertoire of the interviewer during the second stage of the funnelling process, as illustrated in figure 6.2. Summarizing and checking understanding, on the other hand, occur more frequently at the closing-down phase of funnelling through each topic under discussion.

By summarizing and checking understanding the interviewer is attempting to re-state ground already covered in the interview, but also to obtain the candidate's confirmation of their understanding. For example:

Interviewer: *'So, let me summarize so far.* You said you were sales support director for Bloggs Industrial Holdings between February 1992 and March 1993, and that you were responsible for over seventy staff in that department.'

Candidate: 'Yes, that's right.'

Alternatively, summarizing/checking understanding is useful to allow the interviewee to correct any misunderstandings:

Interviewer: *'So, just to check my own understanding* of your responsibilities in your present job. You are a semi-skilled machine tool operator responsible for setting up the CNC lathe for operation.'

Candidate: 'Well, not just setting up the lathe, but checking tolerances on machined tools against MOD specifications. It is graded as a skilled machinists job by the AUEW.'

Behaviour description-type (BD) questions

Patterned Behaviour Description Interviews (PBDIs) were described in some detail in chapter 4. A PBDI procedure requires in-depth critical incident job analysis to be conducted in order to establish the behavioural dimensions against which to rate candidate's replies to questions (Janz, et al., 1986). It is possible, however, to utilize BD-type questions in a less structured manner in circumstances where an organization is genuinely unable or unwilling to move to fully fledged PBDIs. A few examples are as follows:

'I can appreciate that some of your responsibilities in your last job as retail sales assistant are directly comparable with ones you will have to deal with in our sales outlets. Can you think of an instance when you were dealing with a difficult customer who was angry and dissatisfied with their purchase? *Describe exactly what you did and you went about solving this situation.*'

'As police constable in the Metropolitan Police Service, I'm sure you had to face a few dangerous situations. Of course, this could also be true of you become a security guard within our company. You think of a situation where you came up against a potentially violent member of the public as a police officer. *Describe to me the situation and precisely what you did to deal with this person?*'

Situational-type questions

We also described situational interviews more fully in chapter 4. Again, however, it is possible to use elements of this approach without moving to the highly structured format demanded by situational interviews proper. Recalling the style of questioning applied in situational interviews, it will be remembered that the thrust of each question, is 'What would you do in this situation?'
Several examples are given in chapter 4, so just a couple will suffice here:

'In the job which you have applied for as security guard, you can sometimes come up against a potentially violent situation. *What would you do if* a group of three men surrounded you while you were delivering valuable company cheques to be banked at the end of a busy day?'

'From your BTEC in Design I'm sure you realize that a technical designer often needs to show a flair for creativity. *If I asked you to* design an innovative glazing system for the building we are now sitting in, *how would you go about doing this?*'

For both situational-type questions and BD questions there is nothing to preclude the interviewer asking these as part of an ordinary semi-structured or focused interview. It is advisable though, to base such questioning strategies upon detailed critical incident job analysis and the other components of fully fledged PBDIs and situational interviews.

Inadvisable Techniques

A few interviewers apparently believe their own style of social interaction to be so proficient as to render them exempt from needing professional advice regarding their questioning strategies. Hence the preponderance of inadvisable techniques encountered by anyone applying for jobs and attending interviews. The range of inadvisable question types spans from the simply invaluable, to the misleading, to the offensive, to the discriminatory and illegal.

Closed questions

Closed questions are the type that require only a one-word or very short answer. They act as factual checks and, although for most of the time are not of much value to the interviewer, they can occasionally be useful to confirm understanding of specific points. For instance:

'So you left school with nine GCSEs all at grade A?'

'From what you were saying, your present job involves supervising four people in the financial accounts section?'

Leading questions

Leading questions provide the candidate with little or no room for manoeuvre, by setting up only one obvious answer. An example might be:

'You don't mind if I talk now about your present job, do you?'

'Clearly, being able to deal with people is an important part of a bank clerk's job. Do you feel you can do this?'

Not only will the information received by the interviewer from leading questions be highly predictable, it can often be misleading since the recruiter has to some extent forced this reply upon the candidate. Leading questions should therefore be avoided.

Dysfunctional sidertracking

Dysfunctional sidetracking is where the interviewer misdirects the candidate into an irrelevant or inappropriate topic for questioning and, by so doing, loses the thread of the interaction. In the authors' experience, dysfunctional sidetracking occurs with striking regularity in selection interviews. Take, for example, the following instances, based upon actual recruitment interviews:

Example A: Graduate trainee applicant

Candidate: 'I studied Management Sciences at university and specialized in Marketing and Personnel Management. My project was in the area of staff selection, particularly interview techniques.'

Interviewer: 'So, I should be careful in my style of interviewing. Go on then, give me marks out of ten for my performance so far!'

Example B: Production director applicant

Interviewer: 'I notice you list your hobbies as golf and squash. I'm a keen golfer myself. Where do you play and what is your handicap?'

Applicant: 'Well, to be honest I have been so busy with end-of-year stocktaking in the production department that I have not been able to fit a round in for months.'

Interviewer: 'But when you do manage to, where do you tend to play?'
(probing)

Given the ever-present temptation for interviewers to follow up an area of personal interest, care has to be taken not to ask questions which are dysfunctional (i.e., which provide no data relevant to the job in hand), or which sidetrack the candidate away from the topic under consideration.

Personally intrusive questions

More damaging are questions which intrude into the applicant's personal life and which have no bearing on their performance in their job of work. Avoid questions which probe into the candidate's:

- family background and history
- political views and opinions. This is especially fashionable among graduate recruiters, but probably has little or no relevance to actual job performance.
- marital status and plans – particularly as such questions may well be deemed discriminatory and an infringement of equal opportunities legislation (see chapter 8 for further details).
- leisure activities. Again, are such questions relevant?[3]

Discriminatory questions

Many interviewers continue to ask questions which are directly or indirectly discriminatory and therefore illegal. A few do so knowingly in an attempt to flaunt the spirit of the law for whatever reason. Most do so unwittingly, but could nevertheless be held liable by an industrial tribunal. We come on to deal with this legislative framework as it relates to selection interviews in chapter 8.

To summarize the range of questioning strategies open to the interviewer – there is clearly more to asking questions than simply asking questions! Valuable techniques include open and probing questions, reflection, and summarizing/checking understanding. Questions to avoid include closed or leading questions, those which mislead the interaction or are personally intrusive to the candidate, and, at the very extreme, those which are discriminatory under current equal opportunities statutes. To conclude this section, case example 6.2 sets out the opening stages of two parallel selection interviews. The first is conducted by an interviewer who is unskilled in questioning strategies, the second by a recruiter with considerable skill in this area. The case is intended to illustrate the demonstrable differences in the information elicited by each interviewer.

Case Example 6.2

Skilled and unskilled interviewer questioning strategies

Interview A: The unskilled interviewer

Interviewer (I):	'Thanks for coming for interview today. Did you manage to find us alright?' (*social pleasantry*)
Candidate (C):	'Yes, no problems really.'
I:	'So, let me work through your application. You don't mind do you if I go through it section by section?' (*closed question, but does request permission*)
C:	'No, that's fine.'
I:	'I note from your application that you left school with two 'A' Levels?' (*leading question, restating the obvious*)
C:	'Yes, that's right.'
I:	'You left to become an administration assistant with Bowens Industries in their marketing department?' (*closed question*)

C:	'Yes, that's right. It seemed like a good career opportunity.'
I:	'What did your mother and father feel about this?' (*dysfunctional sidetracking – irrelevant data requested*)
C:	'Oh, I think they supported me quite well. I was living at home, so I was able to talk with them quite a lot.'
I: (interrupting)	'You were still living with your parents when you were 20 years old?' (*dysfunctional sidetracking, moral judgement, and closed question*)
C:	'Yes, that's right. I felt . . .'
I (interrupting):	'So, your job in marketing involved the usual kinds of things – sales support, advertising, and so on – I take it.' (*assumption, leading question*)
C:	'Yes, well, I suppose so. It also involved a lot of direct contact with our customers.'

Interview B: The skilled interviewer

I:	'Thanks for coming for interview today. Did you manage to find us alright?' (*soical pleasantry*)
C:	'Yes, no problems really.'
I:	'So, thanks for taking the trouble to send me your application. If its O.K. with you, we can firstly spend some time to work through it section by section, and then leave some time for me to answer any questions you may want to ask me. Is that alright?' (*sets the scene, requests permission to develop rapport*)
C:	'Yes, that's fine.'
I:	'I notice from your application that you chose to do english language and geography 'A' Levels at school. Tell me about your reasons for choosing these subjects.' (*open question, easy question at start to relax candidate*)
C:	'Well, there were several reasons really. I enjoyed English most of all at GCSE, particularly the styles of composition that we had to practise for assignment work. With geography, I thought as my marks at GCSE were always good that I should carry on because I could do it quite easily really.'
I:	'So, you enjoyed English most of all but thought you were best in geography?' (*reflection, checking understanding*)
C:	'Yes, exactly. My real talents, I think, were to do with geography. But I tried exceptionally hard on my English work and improved my own skills,

especially in business report writing and letter writing skills. I practised a lot in my own time.'

I: 'O.K. . . . So you then left to become administration assistant with Bowens Industries in their marketing department. What were your reasons for choosing this route?' (*open question, opening up topic area*)

C: 'Well, it seemed to be a good career opportunity. The job involved a lot of the skills in use of English that I had practised as part of my 'A' Levels. It also involved a lot of contact with all sorts of people which was what I wanted – to move away from academic studies into the real world of work.'

I: 'Uh, uh. That's interesting.' (*positive reinforcement*) 'Tell me more about your job duties.' (*open question*)

Questions

1 List the differences between the two interviews.
2 Can you identify specific items of data elicited by interviewer B which remained unknown to interviewer A?
3 How might each interview have progressed after these opening stages?
4 What impression of the organization would you have at this point if you were the interviewee in each scenario?

Interviewer Social skills (cont.)

Note-taking

The fifth component of the social skills model outlined at the start of this chapter is that of note-taking during the interview. The skill here is to take sufficient notes to act as an *aide memoir* for the recruiter after the interview, but not to appear to the interviewee to be doing so. Short one-liners are usually enough, and some interviewers prefer to develop more of a graphical layout of notes over the page by linking together comments with arrows and by circling around sets of comments perceived to be related in some way.

Every interviewer has their own method of note-taking. Most accomplished recruiters prefer not to scribble notes frantically, but to wait for an appropriate moment and then summarize the key points so far. Whatever style of note-taking is used, 'practice makes perfect', and it will certainly benefit the less experienced interviewer to consciously develop and improve their own style during the early part of their career as a recruiter.

Closing down

The sixth and final element of our model for successful selection interviewing is that of being able to close-down the interview by bringing it to a satisfactory parting. The more experienced interviewer will be conversant with the two common types of strategy for achieving this which can be illustrated by the following examples:

1 *Thanks and we will let you know*, i.e.
  'Well, Mr Withington, thanks for taking the trouble to come and talk with us today. We are seeing other candidates over the rest of today and tomorrow and should be able to let you know one way or the other within about a fortnight.'
2 *Where do we go from here?*, i.e.
  'So, I think we have covered everything I wanted to today. Unless you have any other questions, what will happen next is that I will give your application some further thought and then get back in touch with you. If you are shortlisted I will invite you back for the two day assessment centre which is the next stage of the selection process.'

Having described in some depth the six components of our social skills model for successful interviewing, we should add a couple of caveats to this model in practice before we move on to consider this approach from the perspective of the interviewee.

The first is that 'putting it all together' requires a considerable amount of practice and training support. Interviewing is a high level social skill and good interviewers are developed not born. Combing the six components of the model – (1) rapport development, (2) empathic listening, (3) process management, (4) questioning strategies, (5) note-taking, and (6) closing-down – into a fluent, articulate, convincing and effective performance by the interviewer may take several years to perfect.

There is a second caveat. These skills relate solely to the social-domain skills of interviewing. There can be no guarantee that, having demonstrated all of these skills in abundance, the interviewer will reach a correct outcome decision to accept or reject a candidate. Referring back to our cognitive-social model of successful selection interviewing propounded in chapter 5, figure 5.1, the

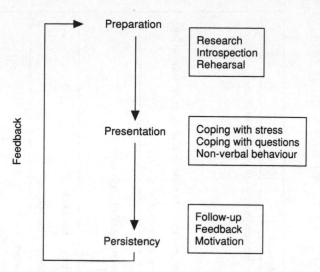

Figure 6.2 The social skills of successful interviewees – the PPP model.

information processing and decision making tasks of the interviewer are essentially cognitive, rather than social, in nature. One thing is sure, however. By using these social skills to their full potential the interviewer will maximize their chances of eliciting accurate and comprehensive information from the candidate upon which to reach their outcome decision.

Interviewee Social Skills

Is there an equivalent social skills model for successful interviewee performance? Well, some of the components of our social skills model for recruiters are clearly specific to the job demands of, and the situation power vested in, the interviewer. For example, probing questions, leading the interaction, and deciding when to draw the interview to a close are all prerogatives enjoyed by the interviewer.

The interviewee, on the other hand, has to influence the process in more subtle ways in an attempt to maximize their chance of success. A few years ago the first author, while involved in conducting skills training for interviewees returning to the job market, developed such a model, termed the 'Preparation-Presentation-Persistency' or 'PPP' model. Based upon earlier and much more detailed work by Professor Clive Fletcher at the University of London (Fletcher, 1981), figures 6.2 and 6.3 summarize the PPP

Phase	Activity	Advice to interviewees
Preparation	Research	Conduct an all-encompassing search of media likely to carry job opportunities in your career area. Indentify all opportunities. Screen opportunities into • most desired and suitable • possibly desired and suitable • outlyers but still possible Submit applications, taking care not to give any reason for organizations to reject you while giving them every reason to want to follow up your application. Research company history, products, market and job vacancy applied for.
	Introspection	Consider the critical questions: • Why should the organization appoint you and not one of the many other applicants? • What are the strenghts and weakness of your application? • What questions might be posed at the interview?
	Rehearsal	Go through a role play scenario of the interview for the vacancy in question. Modify your performance based upon constructive feedback. Identify weaknesses in your style, both verbal and non-verbal (see below).
Presentation	Coping with stress	The interview, like any other presentation, is a stressful situation. Have confidence to deal with anxiety – it is only natural at this stage. Open the interview well – appear assertive and confident, but not brash. Try to settle your early nerves – interviewers will make allowances for this.

Figure 6.3 Components of the PPP social skills model.

Coping with questions		Answer questions directly – do not waffle. It is best not to try to answer factual questions to which you genuinely do not know the answer – admit this to be the case. Be honest but 'economical with the truth' – i.e., put yourself forward in the best possible light without resorting to deception. Do not be provoked – abusive questions are the sign of an unprofessional interviewer, not that you have blown your chances of success.
Non-verbal behaviour		Non-verbal behaviour (NVB), or body language, is an important determinant of interviewer decisions. Consider your: • posture – relaxed but attentive • eye contact – look at the interviewer for most of the time and hold eye contact • facial expressions – do not be afraid to smile occasionally • gestures – an over-animated gestural style is off-putting • head nods – useful to signal empathic listening to the interviewer when they are talking
Persistency	Follow-up	If you do not hear from the organization in a reasonable period of time, politely chase them up. If you are not successful on this occasion, ask for feedback as to why not.
	Feedback	Assimilate this feedback into your next application process and interview performance. Consider any other implications of this feedback for your preparation prior to interview.
	Motivation	Applying for any job carries a 'psychological investment' – that is, you commit not only time and trouble to the process but also your thoughts, feelings, emotions and ambitions. Being unsuccessful is therefore a setback – your psychological investment has, on this occasion, not paid dividends. Rationalize this by not letting it influence your motivation negatively – one common strategy is to find fault in the organization's selection procedure, especially the interview!

Figure 6.3 (cont'd)

- One in five candidates admitted to being 'seldom, or never, completely honest' during interviews.
- Conversely, almost four out of five believed that the candidate should 'sell themself as being the right person for the job'.
- One in three stated that the candidate should try to project a particular 'image' of the sort of person they would like the interviewer to think they were.
- Only a modest 71 per cent agreed that it is 'best to be completely honest with the interviewer'.

Figure 6.4   Troublesome findings from recent research into candidate impression management.
Sources (1)   C. Fletcher, *Personnel Management*, March 1992; (2)   C. Fletcher, *Personnel Review, 10*, No 3, 1981.

model as a cyclical skills model for dealing with the process of applying for jobs and attending interviews.

The model was developed as a highly practical tool for assisting candidates applying for jobs and being invited for interview by organizations. Our 'points of advice' to interviewees given in figure 6.3 are intended to facilitate introspection and improvement in self-presentation over a number of interviews. These points are derived from recent research into what has been referred to as *'impression management techniques'* (Giacalone and Rosenfield, 1991).

Impression management techniques

All interviewees use impression management techniques, it is just that some do so knowingly and some do so better than others. This is an important point to make at the outset, since many recruiters we have spoken with are surprised to find that occupational psychologists are willing to conduct impression management training for interviewees. The common response from recruiters is that 'surely this must be unethical, immoral or unprofessional?' The answer is quite the opposite. We would retort with several arguments:

● Recruiters are already up against candidates who are experienced, and sometimes trained, impression managers. Do interviewers really believe that skilful candidates are not intentionally 'faking-good' or being 'economical with the truth'? Those who do should consult figure 6.4.

- Impression management training works – candidates can, and are, being trained to significantly improve their style of self-presentation to maximize their chances of success at interview.
- Interviewers are sometimes influenced too greatly by impression management skills. For instance, in job roles which do not demand these inter-personal skills the interviewer needs to be careful not to allow them to bias their ratings of candidate suitability too heavily.
- Training candidates who are less skilful at self-presentation merely evens out differences between those who are naturally skilled and those whose skills need developing.
- Given the susceptibility of recruiters to 'primacy effect' (i.e., the first few minutes of the interview being most influential), and 'confirmatory information seeking bias' (i.e., actively seeking information to confirm early impressions (see chapter 3 for further details) candidates may only need to impression manage effectively very early on in the interview. And, perhaps, most contentious of all . . .
- Training interviewees in impression management techniques promises to improve interviewer performance as well! Faced with trained and skilled candidates, it is a safe bet that interviewers will respond (or will have to), and that, in the longer term, interviewing practices will improve all round.

Concluding Comments

In this chapter we have put forward a social skills approach to the roles of the interviewer and the interviewee. It is axiomatic to conceive of the interview as a social encounter, but it is also one which is notably unusual in its purpose and interactional processes. The extent to which the interviewer and the interviewee are socially skilled in their interactional styles will determine how successful is their meeting. In conclusion, interviews provide precisely that – an opportunity for an 'inter-view' between both parties. Developing skilled strategies in both roles is an important precursor to being a successful proponent either as an interviewer or as a candidate.

Summary Propositions

1 Successful selection interviewing depends on possessing and applying high level social skills to elicit accurate and comprehensive information from the candidate.
2 Interviewer social skills comprise:
   (a) rapport development
   (b) empathic listening

    (c)   process management
    (d)   questioning strategies
    (e)   note-taking
    (f)   closing-down
3 Rapport development and empathic listening skills involve both verbal and non-verbal components.
4 Process management skills can be sub-divided into *funnelling* and *pacing*, with each topic moving through three phases:
    (a)   opening up,
    (b)   probing
    (c)   closing-down and moving on
5 Effective questioning strategies include:
    (a)   open questions
    (b)   probing questions
    (c)   reflection
    (d)   summarizing/checking understanding
    (e)   Behaviour Description-type questions
    (f)   situational-type questions
6 Successful candidates at interview show skills of:
    (a)   Preparation
    (b)   Presentation
    (c)   Persistency
7 Interviewees use a variety of impression management techniques in order to maximize their chances of success at interview.

Notes

1 See also V. J. Shackleton (1989) *How to Pick People for Jobs* (London: Fontana).
2 See also O. Hargie, C. Saunders and D. Dickson (1987) *Social Skills in Interpersonal Communication*, Second edition (Beckenham: Croom Helm).
3 For a recent survey into candidate's views of such question areas consult C. Fletcher (1992) Ethics & the job interview, *Personnel Management*, March 1992, 36–9.

References

Argyle, M. (1983) *The Psychology of Interpersonal Behaviour* (Harmondsworth: Penguin).

Farr, R. (1982) Interviewing: the social psychology of the interview, in A. J. Chapman and A. Gale (eds) *Psychology and People* (London: BPS/Macmillan).

Fletcher, C. (1981) *Facing the Interview* (London: Unwin Paperbacks).

Giacalone, R. A. and Rosenfield, P. (eds) (1991) *Applied Impression Management* (London: Sage).

Janz, T., Hellervik, L. and Gilmore, D. C. (1986) *Behavior Description Interviewing: New Accurate, Cost-Effective* (Boston: Allyn & Bacon Inc).

Kahn, R. L. and Cannell, C. F. (1960) *The Dynamics of Interviewing: Theory, Technique, and Cases* (New York: John Wiley).

Millar, R. Crute, V. and Hargie, O. (1992) *Professional Interviewing* (London: Routledge).

Morris, D., Collett, P., Marsh, P. and O'Shaughnessy, M. (1979) *Gestures: Their Origins and Distribution* (New York: Cape).

7
Interview Skills III: Decision Making

'The function of the interviewer is to secure information, evaluate it, and come to a final decision. The evaluated items of information are somehow summated or integrated to arrive at this decision, the essential nature of which is to accept or reject.'

Springbett, *Factors affecting the final decision in the employment interview*, 1958

Decisions, Decisions . . .

In this chapter we turn our focus toward the decision making skills of successful selection interviewing. We thus build on the review of interview research undertaken in chapter 3 and the preceding two chapters in this part of the book which discussed interview preparation and the social skills of information elicitation. The focus in this chapter, though, is upon the pragmatic concerns of reaching accurate outcome decisions. Specifically, we consider four key questions:

- How best can interviewers combine so many pieces of information about the candidate to arrive at a hiring decision?
- How should interviewers allocate weights as to the importance of each piece of emergent data?
- How much credence should be given to the interview relative to other assessment techniques in final decision making?
- What tools and techniques are there available to the interviewer to assist in their day-to-day task of decision making?

As we pointed out in our cognitive-social model of interview decision making (chapter 5, figure 5.1), the recruiter is charged with several major responsibilities:

- the evaluate each item of information;
- to allocate it an appropriate weight in decision making;
- to combine multiple sources of data; in order
- to reach a final accept-reject decision.

On Signs and Samples of Behaviour

In a now classic paper on selection decision making published in the American Journal of Applied Psychology in 1968, Paul Wernimont and John Campbell drew an important distinction between what they termed 'signs' and 'samples' of behaviour (Wernimont and Campbell, 1968). In the context of the interview, a sign would be a single behaviour by the candidate, say one particular reply or one striking non-verbal behaviour such as avoiding eye contact at a crucial moment. Samples, on the other hand, are 'collections' of similar behaviours which are grouped together according to justifiable logic.

As one might expect, the research shows unequivocally that predicting future job performance from individual signs of behaviour is a notoriously risky business. In other words, if it works it only does so purely by chance. Unfortunately, the number of interviewers willing and ready to engage in such a risky strategy shows little prospect of diminishing. Over the years the authors have spoken with countless interviewers in various industries each possessing their own 'failsafe' method of spotting poor candidates. These include:

- *the limp handshake* – attributed to be a sign of personality weakness, even in female candidates (or, indeed, in those with a weaker grip).
- *white socks* – one interviewer was adamant that wearing white socks to an interview was a blatant sign of homosexuality. In his words 'homosexuality has no place in the British armed forces.'
- *stooping posture* – candidates seen to be stooping too far forward were reported by one interviewer as being rejected automatically as too subservient.
- *the 'magic question'* – many interviewers continue to rely upon this approach. Biding their time, they spring forth with their one 'magic question' sworn to discriminate between high flyers and also-rans.
- *deviant non-verbals* – a few examples include: shifty eyes as a sign of dishonesty; scratching one's nose as a sign of lying; fidgeting as a sign of hyperactivity; and so forth.

- *class background* – one personnel manager formerly known to one of the authors was infamous for shortlisting, not upon the achievements or personality of candidates, but upon the socio-economic class background of their parents. Those below professional-managerial class were rejected out-of-hand.

This catalogue of idiosyncratic decision making strategies, relying upon signs of candidate behaviour, would be amusing if it was not for the fact that these are real-life examples of interviewers reaching expensive employment decisions which effect the future course of the candidate's career and lifestyle. The point is that *samples not signs of behaviour need to be the basis of interviewer decisions*, and that decisions need to be reached in an *objective rather than a subjective way*. Our intention in this chapter is to describe some of the ways in which this can be accomplished.

Candidate Assessment Typologies

Perhaps the most popular method of imposing some objectivity upon interviewer decision making is to use a standardized candidate assessment typology. Two such typologies are in widespread use in industry today:

- Rodger's (1952) seven-fold framework; and
- Munro Fraser's (1978) five-point plan.

The seven-fold framework

Originally proposed in 1952, Professor Alec Rodger's (1952) seven-fold framework is possibly still the most widely used typology. Many interviewer training courses are built around this system of evaluation which probably remains popular due to its comprehensive coverage of factors, and because of its ease of use. Interviewees are rated against seven dimensions:

1 *Physical make up* – appearance, dress, physical health;
2 *Attainments* – general education, vocational training, professional qualifications, career attainments;
3 *General intelligence* – overall cognitive ability measured as the 'g' factor in psychometric tests of intelligence;
4 *Special aptitudes* – specific abilities and attainments;

5   *Interests* – spare time activities, sports, hobbies, etc;
6   *Disposition* – personality, reliability, acceptability to others;
7   *Circumstances* – family life, home circumstances, general way of life.

The five-point plan

In 1957 John Munro Fraser (1978) from Aston University, Birmingham, began work to improve the seven-fold framework. He condensed Rodger's seven original dimensions into five factors and advocated the use of a twenty-point grading system across these dimensions. The factors comprising his five-point plan are:

1   *Impact on others* – appearance, speech and manner, health.
2   *Qualifications and experience* – general education, vocational training, etc;
3   *Innate abilities* – verbal, perceptual, numerical, mechanical, spatial;
4   *Motivation* – level of goals, realism and consistency in following them up;
5   *Emotional adjustment* – acceptability, sense of responsibility, reliability and leadership.

The twenty-point grading system proposed by Munro Fraser is illustrated in figure 7.1. The system relies upon classifying candidates against the spread of individuals in the population as a normal distribution across five grades, sub-divided into twenty further grading points.

Figure 7.2 shows this grading system in usage for a fairly senior level managerial vacancy.

Referring to figure 7.2, it is apparent that James Holloway, the candidate for this vacancy, is seen by the interviewer as a strong possibility in this recruitment process. Ratings fall mostly in the A grade, or the top ten per cent of the population, and only the rating for performance on the numerical ability test has given this interviewer some cause for concern. Overall, this example illustrates a completed rating form for a successful candidate where the interviewer's recommendation is to invite the interviewee back for an assessment centre.

Evaluating the typologies: good and bad

Both the seven-fold framework and the five-point plan have strengths and weaknesses. Their strengths are that they:

Grade	Distribution of the population	Ratings
A	Top 10% of the population	17 to 20
B	Upper 20% of the population	13 to 16
C	Middle 40% of the population	9 to 12
D	Lower 20% of the population	5 to 8
E	Bottom 10% of the population	1 to 4

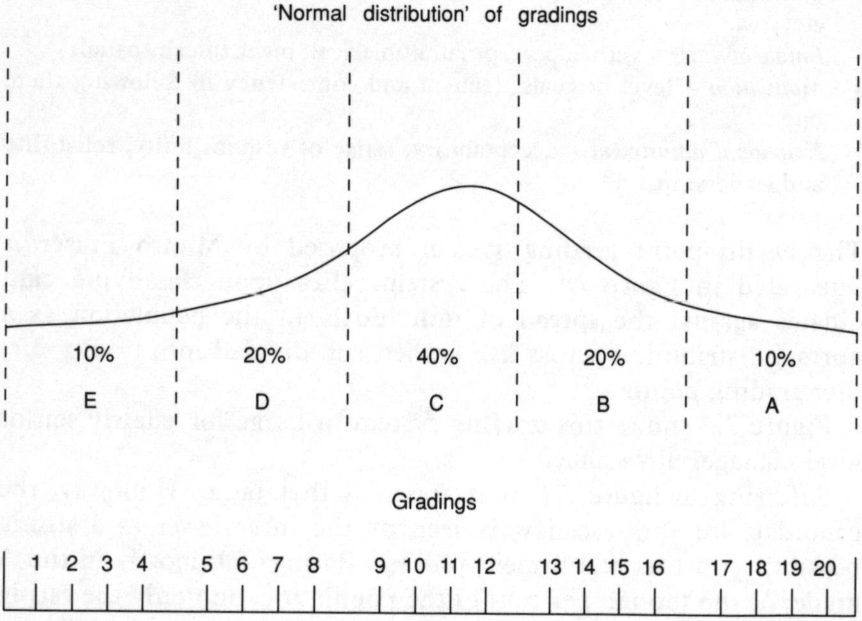

'Normal distribution' of gradings

Figure 7.1 Gradings in the five-point plan.

- are easy to understand and apply with minimal interviewer training;
- impose parameters and categories onto interviewers' ratings, thus forcing interviewers to rate against predefined criteria; and so
- are a considerable improvement upon rating procedures where no predefined criteria are established.

	E Grade\nBottom 10%	D Grade\nLower 20%	C Grade\nMiddle 40%	B Grade\nUpper 20%	A Grade\nTop 10%	Interviewer's comments
Scale	1 2 3	4 5 6 7 8	9 10 11 12 13	14 15 16	17 18 19 20	
Impact on others					18	Smart, well-groomed, likely to create good first impressions in others.
Qualifications and experience				16		Honours degree in Business Studies. Supervisory experience of twelve months over six clerical staff.
Innate abilities\n• verbal\n• numerical		numerical 4	verbal 9			Test scores indicate only moderate levels of cognitive ability. Verbal test score somewhat below average. Numerical test score only average.
Motivation				16		Has achieved targets set in school and university; future aims realistic and achievable. Appears to have high internal motivation for this vacancy.
Emotional adjustment				16		Stable and reliable. Consistent pattern of leadership positions in school, university and industry. Trustworthy.

Candidate: James Holloway
Position: Management Executive – Sales Department
Recommendation: Invite for assessment centre. Excellent candidate overall. Numerical ability needs ratifying.

Figure 7.2 Example of the five-point plan in use.

Against these advantages stand a number of disadvantages:

● the typologies *assume* all interviewers can use the dimensions in the same way and that the dimensions are appropriate for all types of job function;
● evaluations may be *objectified subjectivity* with interviewer ratings still being prone to the many errors of subjectivity outlined in chapter 3;
● dimensions carry *equal weight* in outcome decisions – different jobs will probably require differential weighting procedures.

So, are the typologies useful in employee selection? The answer is a qualified 'yes'. At the very least these typologies offer 'ready-made' criteria against which to assess candidates. The categories are necessarily broad to permit interviewers to rate on these typologies for a range of job functions. Broadness may imply vagueness, however, and there is the possibility that interviewers each interpret the dimensions quite differently to one another.

More important is the criticism that the dimensions comprising these typologies, as they were originally published, all carry equal weights in outcome decisions. For example, in figure 7.2 all but two of the ratings given were in the 'A' or 'B' grades, that is, in the top ten per cent or next twenty per cent of the population. The only evaluations to fall below this were those allocated to the cognitive ability tests, where both results are described as only 'average' or 'somewhat below average'. The problem here is that this job, management executive in the sales department, involves constant use of numerical and written data, including hand calculations, interpretation of data, and the reaching of decisions based upon these interpretations. Such activities are critical to the successful performance of this job function, and so these two cognitive ability tests are likely to be highly predictive of future on-the-job performance.

What is needed, therefore, is a method of weighting the relative importance of each dimension for different job functions. Two ways of doing this exist:

● statistical weighting algorithms; and
● visual-perceptual algorithms.

1 *Statistical weighting algorithms* Under a statistical weighting procedure, a statistical algorithm is used to standardize decision making based on differential weights for each dimension in the typology. There are several ways of doing this, but the principle remains the same – to allocate appropriate weights to each dimension relative to the demands of the job being recruited for.

Perhaps the most easy to understand algorithm is where unity, or 1.0, is taken as the base-line weighting, with deviations from this weighting being allocated on some justifiable basis. The extremes of this algorithm are 0.5 as the lowest weighting and 1.5 as the highest weighting.

Again, using our evaluation of James Holloway, the candidate in figure 7.2, we demonstrate this algorithm for statistical weighing in table 7.1.

There are several advantages in using a statistically weighted decision making procedure in this way. As we show in table 7.1, those dimensions which should exert greater influence upon outcome decisions (here, Abilities and Motivation) actually do so. In this case the weighting procedure may well have toned down the interviewer's final comments compared to those made in figure 7.2, where the interviewer seems to have been unduly influenced by the less important assessment dimensions. The second advantage is that dimensions affect decisions in a consistent manner if the same algorithm is applied to all candidates. This is an important advantage since the algorithm minimizes any unreliability in interviewer decision making, especially any variations across candidates. Given the susceptibility of interviewers to such variations[1] (see chapter 3 for a detailed review of the research evidence), it is clear that using standardized algorithm confers most useful benefits.

2   *Visual-perceptual algorithms*   The second method for weighting dimensions can be termed the *visual-perceptual* method. Here, the rating form is designed in such a way as to provide visual cues as to the relative importance of each dimension. Using our example assessments in figure 7.2 and table 7.1, we show the use of a visual-perceptual rating form in figure 7.3.

Once again, the aim is to allow those dimensions which are most predictive of success on-the-job to influence the interviewer's decision most heavily. The difference with a statistical weighting procedure is that visual-perceptual weighting relies upon the visual and cognitive impact of the layout of the form. In this example we have actually sized the candidate assessment boxes proportionate to the weightings in the statistical algorithm. Again, though, figure 7.3 illustrates the relative impact of highly important dimensions such as Abilities compared with those of less import such as Qualifications.

Table 7.1 An illustration of statistically weighted decision making procedures

Dimension	Job-relevance	Weight	Candidate grading	Weight × grading
Impact on others	Limited to internal contact with colleagues within the organization. Average importance compared with other executive grade jobs.	1.00	18	18.00
Qualifications	Not particularly important or a prerequisite for this job.	0.50	17	8.50
Abilities	Of over-riding importance. Data handling and interpretation are core elements of this job function.	1.50	An average of $(5 + 9)/2 = 14/2 = 7$	10.50
Motivation	Highly important. Candidate needs to have the highest motivation to perform, and dedication to the organization.	1.25	20	25.00
Emotional adjustment	Not of particular import. As long as no real grounds for concern arise. This factor is not that crucial.	0.75	16	12.00
Grand Total				74.00

Dimension	Job relevance	Interviewer's comments		Grading assessment
Impact on others	Limited to internal contact with colleagues within the organization. Average importance compared with other executive grade jobs.	Smart, well-groomed, likely to create good first impressions in others.		18
Qualifications	Not particularly important or a prerequisite for this job.	Horours degree in Business Studies. Supervisory experience of twelve months over six clerical staff.		17
Abilities	Of over-riding importance. Data handling and interpretation are core elements of this job function.	Test scores indicate only moderate levels of cognitive ability. Verbal test score somewhat below average. Numerical test score only average.	Verbal 5 → 7 Numerical 9	20
Motivation	Highly important. Candidate needs to have the highest motivation to perform, and dedication to the organization.	Has achieved targets set in school and university. Future aims realistic and achievable. Appears to have high internal motivation for this vacancy.		
Emotional adjustment	Not of particular import. As long as no real grounds for concern arise, this factor is not that crucial.	Stable and reliable. Consistent pattern of leadership positions in school, university and industry. Trustworthy.		16

Figure 7.3 Visual-perceptual rating form.

Dimension Weightings

Both the statistical and the visual-perceptual methods represent distinct improvements over standardized assessment typologies where no account is taken of weighting different dimensions for different jobs. But, how should these weights be established in the first place?

This is the point at which we need to return to our systems of selection perspective advocated in chapter 2. By viewing interview decision making as only part of an on-going systematic procedure in this way, interview decisions, and therefore the weights given to each assessment dimension, stand in relation to other phases in the system. At the very minimum, dimension weights need to be derived from accurate and up-to-date job analysis as we described in chapter 2. It is only by being sure of the task elements comprising the job, and of the concomitant skills needed to perform these tasks, that appropriate weights can be allocated to dimensions. It is also important to note that this process is iterative and on-going. That is, once weightings have been derived from job analysis they need to be validated against subsequent performance appraisal data.[2] Jobs change and it is therefore important for the recruiter not to overlook this process of securing feedback on both their interview decisions and on their candidate assessment procedures. This is essentially a statistical and empirical question which is driven by the question 'does the decision making algorithm work as well as possible?'

Combining Assessments from Multiple Techniques

Although perhaps the majority of organizations still rely on the interview supplemented with a simple reference check to reach selection decisions, a growing number are using more objective and sophisticated techniques (Shackleton and Newell, 1991). And quite rightly so, as we argued in chapters 2 and 3. The difficulty for those using multiple assessment techniques is to combine all the ratings given to dimensions on each technique into an overall *select* or *reject* decision.

Of course, this is not a new problem (Feltham, 1989). Indeed, for recruiters experienced in running assessment centres, where several methods are used over one or more days, this is an old chestnut. Combining assessments of each candidate across dimensions as rated in each selection method is no easy task. In some circumstances we can be looking to combine dozens of individual assessment ratings. It is thus just as important to establish an algorithm to combine these data at this overarching level as it is to combine dimension evaluations in the interview. Again, either a statistical or a visual-perceptual approach can be taken, this time with different weights being allocated to the different techniques utilized (interview, psychometric tests, work samples, etc.).

In an ideal world these weights would be established by scientific and statistical methodology. A predictive validity study of the whole selection system should be undertaken, and those techniques found to be most predictive of subsequent job performance identified. The extent to which the technique is successful in predicting job performance will govern the weight afforded to it in the decision making algorithm. Unfortunately, selection practices in the UK hardly resemble an ideal world, and even today few organizations bother to validate their decision making procedures.

This is not just unfortunate but undoubtedly very costly as well. Having spent so much money on conducting interviews, tests, and the like, it is essential for recruiters to pressure their organization to undertake a thorough validation study. Not only will properly conducted study pay for itself many times over,[3] its findings will indicate the weightings to be applied in the decision making algorithm to the selection methods used.

Concluding Comments

Decision making, whether in the interview or as the culmination of the entire selection process, is essentially an information processing task. In chapters 2 and 3 we warned of the dangers of information overload in selection – that is, where the recruiter is attempting to process too much information in relation to their cognitive capacities. Resorting to snap judgements, prejudice and bias, or reaching outcome decisions on signs rather than samples of behaviour are far from viable solutions. Quite the opposite. By imposing an objective procedure or algorithm for decision making upon these data the interviewer will at least ensure some degree of reliability. However, only if the algorithm has been properly validated will the recruiter maximize their chance of reaching accurate selection decisions in the longer term.

Summary Propositions

1 Selection decision making by the recruiter is a complex information processing task.
2 Samples, not signs of behaviour, need to constitute the basis of final decisions.
3 Information needs to be evaluated, weighted, and summed in an objective rather than subjective manner to reach outcome decisions.
4 Existing candidate assessment typologies offer 'ready-made' dimensions for evaluation but have several inherent weaknesses.
5 Decisions making algorithms can be based on one of two main weighting procedures:
   (a) statistical weighting
   (b) visual-perceptual weighting
6 Any decision making algorithm should be properly validated through detailed scientific and statistical study.

Notes

1 See also R. D. Arvey and J. E. Campion (1982) The Employment Interview: a summary and review of recent research, *Personnel Psychology*, 35, 281–322.
2 A detailed account is given, for instance, in J. Arnold, I. T. Robertson and C. L. Cooper (1991) *Work Psychology: Understanding Human Behaviour in the Workplace* (London: Pitman) particularly chapters Six and Seven.
3 For example T. Payne, N. R. Anderson, and T. Smith (1992) *Decision Making and Financial Considerations in a Second Generation Assessment Centre*, Paper presented at the BPS Annual Occupational Psychology Conference, Liverpool, January 1992.

References

Feltham, R. T. (1989) Assessment Centres, in P. Herriot (ed.), *Assessment and Selection in Organizations: Methods and Practice for Recruitment and Appraisal* (London: John Wiley).

Munro Fraser, J. (1978) *Employment Interviewing* (London: MacDonald and Evans).

Rodger, A. (1952) *The Seven Point Plan*, National Institute for Industrial Psychology, Paper No. 1.

Shackleton, V. J. and Newell, S. (1991) Management Selection: a comparative survey of methods used in top British & French companies, *Journal of Occupational Psychology*, 64, 23–36.

Springbett, B. M. (1958) Factors Affecting the Final Decision in the Employment Interview, *Canadian Journal of Psychology*, 12, 13–22.

Wernimont, P. F. and Campbell, J. P. (1968) Signs, Samples and Criteria, *Journal of Applied Psychology*, 52, 372–6.

Part III
Interviews in Practice

In part III two issues of particular concern for interviewers are discussed – equal opportunities legislation, and interviewer training and development. These issues are crucial since the anti-discrimination legislation lays down the framework within which selection practices, including interviewing, operate.

Interviewer training, as the issue concerning our final chapter in the book, forms the basis for successful and professional practice. It is therefore appropriate that our final two chapters discuss these issues in some depth.

8
Unfair Discrimination, Equal Opportunities and the Interview

'Employers have also found that, by focusing attention on the treatment of all staff at work, the implementation of equal opportunities policies stimulates a healthy and more productive atmosphere and creates a better quality of working life.'

Guidelines for Equal Opportunities Employers
Equal Opportunities Commission

It is often said that personnel selection, including of course interviewing, aims to discriminate. By this it is meant that selection is about choice. Interviewers aim to try to choose the most suitable candidate or candidates for the job. They try to predict who has the necessary skills, competences, personality, and so on to do a good job and fit into the organization. This approach represents the classical or psychometric tradition in psychology. The negotiation or psychological contract approach places emphasis on the social exchange process, the balance of different forms of power in the interview, the negotiated agreement on whether to select the candidate (or select the job in the case of the applicant) and the sharing of expectations. Yet the social exchange approach is still about discriminating or noting differences between candidates or jobs. And this discrimination made by the selector or interviewer must be made *fairly* (see also chapter 3).

It is easy to find descriptions of fair discrimination or good selection practice. They are contained in codes of practice published by, among others, the Equal Opportunities Commission (EOC) (1985), the Commission for Racial Equality (CRE) (1984), the Institute of Personnel Management (IPM) (1990) and the British Psychological Society (BPS) (1980), and there is also the law.

The two relevant acts in Britain are the 1975 and 1986 Sex Discrimination Acts and the 1976 Race Relations Act. These acts apply not only to recruitment and selection but also to the promotion and transfer of all staff. Employers who contravene the acts are breaking the law and alleged offenders can be brought to industrial tribunals. Both employers and individual employees, such as managers, can be held liable for acts of discrimination. The number of referrals to tribunals and to the courts concerning sex and race discrimination cases varies from year to year, but has increased slightly in recent years. The proportion of successful claims also varies year on year, but tends to be between twenty and twenty-five per cent for sex discrimination claims and ten to twenty per cent for racial claims.

A summary of the scope and principles of the acts follow, but for a fuller account the reader is referred to the Employment Law handbook listed in the references at the end of this chapter.

In this chapter, we will first look at the principles of the acts, and then apply what they have to say to the employment interview.

General Principles of the Acts

The acts are designed to help eliminate discrimination in employment on the grounds of race and sex. They are very similar in their approach and have many provisions in common. In the areas of recruitment and initial appointment they prohibit discrimination:

1   In the arrangements made to decide who will be offered employment (such as different questions asked of a candidate based on race or sex);
2   In the employment terms offered to that person (such as different rates of pay or conditions of work);
3   By refusing or deliberately omitting to offer that person employment (such as deliberately leaving a person off a shortlist because of his or her race or sex).

It is also unlawful to discriminate against an *existing employee* on the grounds of race or sex by:

1   The way opportunities for promotion, transfer, training or other benefits are provided, including deliberately omitting a person access to these (such as providing a particular training course only for whites, which then means that they have better promotion prospects);

2 Dismissals (such as dismissing more female than male workers in a particular job just because they are female);
3 Subjecting a person to any other detriment, that is, anything which is directly or indirectly discriminatory (these are important terms which we will be coming to shortly).

Sex discrimination

According to the Sex Discrimination Act (SDA), discrimination occurs when a woman is treated less favourably than a man because of her sex. The same definition of discrimination broadly applies to men.

The provisions of the act have many practical implications for selectors and interviewers. Employers have to abide by the law at all stages of the process, and especially when:

- deciding on the person specification and pre-screening criteria (see chapter 2)
- drawing up the shortlist
- conducting the interview
- making job offers

All this applies equally to race as well as to sex discrimination.

Fair interviews are those which do not ask discriminatory questions, that is, those which treat a female candidate less favourably than a male.

The following is a list of questions which interviewers might be tempted to use with a female interviewee, but which should be avoided at all cost.

Do you intend to have a family in the near future?
Do you think women are suited to this type of work?
I see you are engaged to be married. Does that mean you will be moving away from the area?
I note that you call yourself Ms. Why is that?
Do you think you would be able to gain the respect of males who report to you?
Are you legally separated?
Have you made arrangements to look after your children while you are at work?
How will you manage if the children are ill?
How will you manage regarding your children if you have to work late unexpectedly?

How would you deal with a man who made it clear that he didn't like
having a woman boss?
How likely is your husband to move his job?
Adapted from *How to Pick People for Jobs*, Viv Shackleton (Fontana, 1989).

The reason these questions, and others like them, are discriminatory is because they are based on stereotyped views of women,
their personalities, their abilities and capabilities, their work and
their lives in general. The interviewer can treat a female candidate
less favourably than a male by assuming, for example, that:

● women cannot gain the respect of male subordinates;
● women are not suited to certain types of work;
● a woman always follows her partner if he gets another job;
● women are the only ones who raise families;
● that men are more likely to be the 'breadwinner';
● the interviewer is discriminating because of the biological fact that
only women give birth.

As a rough and ready guide, interviewers should ask themselves the
question: 'Would I ask this question of a man?' If the answer is 'no',
then they are probably asking a discriminatory question.

Types of discrimination

There are three ways an employer can discriminate under the SDA.
These are:

● direct discrimination
● indirect discrimination
● victimization

1 *Direct discrimination* Direct discrimination occurs when a
person is treated less favourably than others are (or would be) in
similar circumstances, on the grounds of sex or marital status. So, to
refuse to employ a barman because the publican wanted a barmaid
is an example of direct discrimination. In *Munro v Allied Suppliers
(1977)* a man was not appointed as a cook because women employees
would not work with him, and in the case of *Batisha v Say (1977)* a
woman was turned down for a job as a cave guide because it was 'a
man's job'. Industrial tribunals held that both were examples of

direct sex discrimination, since the employer was refusing or deliberately omitting to offer employment because of a person's sex.

2 *Indirect discrimination* Indirect discrimination is described and prohibited under the SDA to tackle more subtle forms of sex discrimination, whether conscious or unconscious. It is indirect discrimination to make an unjustifiable job demand which a smaller proportion of women than men can satisfy. 'Unjustifiable' means that the condition or requirement is not essential to the effective carrying out of the job itself. So an advertisement for 'male or female bar staff, must have a full beard' would be indirect discrimination unless the requirement for a bushy beard is justified.

What has to be considered is whether realistically and *in practice* a woman can comply, not merely theoretically. This thinking lay behind the famous case of *Price v Civil Service Commission (1978)*. The employers made it a requirement that candidates for direct entry to the post of executive officer had to be over the age of seventeen and six months and under twenty-eight. The applicant, Ms Price, was thirty-six. She argued that this requirement amounted to indirect sex discrimination because far fewer women than men could comply with this requirement *in practice*, since many were having or caring for children and so out of the labour market between these ages. The industrial tribunal pointed out that the employer had failed to show that the requirement that candidates were under twenty-eight years of age, irrespective of sex, was justifiable. So *justified* means that the condition should be necessary, not just administratively convenient.

3 *Victimization* An individual can also bring a claim against someone else if she (or he) has been victimized by being treated less favourably than someone else. This victimization can occur when an employee has brought proceedings about, or given evidence on, alleged contravention of the SDA (or the Equal Pay or Race Relations Acts), or intends to do any of these things. This is to protect individuals wanting to bring a case of sex discrimination. However, an individual is protected by the law only if the former allegation of discrimination was 'made in good faith'. 'Acting in good faith' is obviously a grey area and the term is not precisely defined. However, statements made in court by Lord Greene in 1984 can help, even though not made in the context of discrimination.

He stated that a case should not be: 'so absurd that no sensible person could have dreamt that it lay within the powers of the authority. (As an) example . . . the red haired teacher dismissed because she had red hair. It is so unreasonable that it might also be described as being done in bad faith' (Associated Provincial Picture House v Wednesday Corporation (1948)).

Sex discrimination claims based on victimization are fairly rare. But there have been cases, such as where a woman was not considered for promotion because she had threatened to refer her employer's recruitment practices to Advisory, Conciliation and Arbitration Service (ACAS).

Marital status

The SDA covers not only discrimination on the grounds of a person's sex, but also on grounds of marital status. For example, in *North East Midlands Co-operative Society Ltd v Allen (1977)*, the employer had a rule whereby when a female employee married, her original contract of employment ended and a fresh one was issued to her. Mrs Allen was single when she joined the company, and when she married the rule was applied to her. She was offered a different job which she refused to take. So she was dismissed. The tribunal held that this was unlawful discrimination on the grounds of marital status.

A 'marital' discrimination case may also be brought if the employer's policies and procedures have a disproportionately adverse impact on married women. In the case of *Thorndyke v Bell Fruit Ltd (1979)*, Mrs Thorndyke claimed marital discrimination when she was rejected for a job on the grounds that she had young children. The tribunal was provided with evidence showing that the employer was using a criterion that a successful candidate should not have young or dependant children (believing that they were less reliable employees). Married women were disproportionately affected by this policy and Mrs Thorndyke won her case.

The act does not prohibit discrimination on grounds that a person is unmarried. The legislation recognizes that there are certain occupations which are best performed by married couples, such as running a pub, caretaking, or other types of domestic service. The SDA means that it is possible to refuse to engage two single people as compared to a married couple.

Permitted sex discrimination

It is important to note that certain forms of discrimination on the grounds of sex are actually permitted by the SDA, but these categories are strictly limited. The exceptions are where being a man or woman is a 'Genuine Occupational Qualification' (GOQ) or requirement. There are nine categories of permitted GOQ, but in practice examples are few and far between. One is where the job needs to be held by one sex rather than another to preserve decency and privacy. An example is a changing room attendant at a swimming baths. Another is where the nature of the place of work (a hospital or prison, for example) means that supervision of those in care or detention are all of one sex and it is reasonable that the job should not be held by a person of the opposite sex. A final example category is where the job involves duties outside the UK in a country whose laws or customs mean that the duties cannot be effectively performed by one particular sex. This sometimes happens in jobs requiring travel or contact in the Middle East. Further details of GOQs can be found in the texts referred to in the Recommendations for Further Reading in Appendix I.

'Positive discrimination' is not permitted under the SDA. This occurs where one sex is under-represented in a particular job and the employer tries to make a more balanced workforce by discriminating in favour of the minority. In contrast to the USA, there is no 'quota system' in Britain, whereby there must be certain minimum numbers of employees of each sex in certain jobs or grades. Positive discrimination is only permitted in relation to training and then only in certain well-defined circumstances. It is not illegal, though, to encourage applications from the minority sex (in fact the EOC Code of Practice (1985) recommends it) but selection must be on merit without reference to sex.

Race discrimination

Just as with the sex discrimination legislation, the Race Relations Act of 1976 (RRA) makes it unlawful for an employer to treat one applicant less favourably than another, this time on racial grounds. The same goes for existing employees. *Racial* in this context means 'colour, race, nationality, ethnic or national origins'.

Our discussion of the RRA is shorter than that on the SDA, not because it is any less important, but because many of the principles underlying the two acts are the same.

The Commission for Racial Equality (CRE) has, as one of its many functions, the ability to take up cases for individuals, as well as to institute proceedings against employers following CRE investigations. In this sense it is similar to the EOC and, like the EOC, has issued a Code of Practice to help employers and individuals avoid acts of discrimination (see the reference section for details).

There are three ways that employers and individuals can discriminate. These, as with the SDA, are direct discrimination, indirect discrimination, and victimization.

Direct discrimination   Direct discrimination comes about by treating one person less favourably than another on racial grounds. This includes segregating one person from another on grounds of race. This might be when a particular racial group is placed on a shift involving unsocial hours or noisier working conditions than another group. The act also covers cases where an employee is treated unfavourably not because of their own colour or race but on account of the race or colour of someone else. For example, in the case of *Wilson v T B Steelwork Co Ltd (1978)*, an employer refused employment to a white woman because her husband was black. The court found this to be unlawful racial discrimination.

Indirect discrimination   Indirect discrimination is where an employer applies the same requirement to everyone but one racial group is more likely to be able to comply, and the requirement cannot be justified on non-racial grounds. For example, insisting that trainee life assurance salespeople should be at least six foot tall or have blond hair would be indirect racial discrimination, since certain races are much more likely to be able to meet this rule and the rule has no justification. Incidentally, the six foot rule would also be indirect sex discrimination in this case.

The Race Relations Act, just like the Sex Discrimination Act, does allow what might on the surface seem like favourable treatment for one sector of the community. This is only if it is justifiable for the job. So, an employer might be within the lay by insisting that an applicant must speak Urdu, even though less white applicants than Asians would be able to fulfil this particular requirement. This would only be lawful if the job on offer involved extensive work with those speaking Urdu, that is, Asians.

Case law shows that many examples of indirect discrimination have involved rules about clothing and uniforms which disproportionately disadvantage one racial group. Tribunals look to see whether a racial group can comply *in practice* in ways that are consistent with its customs and traditions. In *Mandla v Lee and Park Grove School (1983)*, the school rule was that turbans should not be worn. Although this applied to all pupils, the proportion of Sikhs who could comply was much smaller than the proportion of non-Sikhs. Although Sikhs could remove their turbans, *in practice* to do so would be to go against their cultural traditions. Such a ruling of discrimination would apply equally well in the employment context where there was no non-racial justification.

Discrimination does not have to be intentional to fall foul of the law. Unintentional discrimination can still be unlawful. However, on occasions there may be justification for a ruling even if it has a disproportionate impact on a particular racial group. In *Panesar v The Nestlé* Company (1980), the food factory had a rule prohibiting beards on the grounds of hygiene. Mr Panesar was an orthodox Sikh, so refused to shave off his beard and brought a charge of indirect discrimination. The tribunal accepted medical evidence that there was a hygiene risk from employees wearing beards and dismissed the discrimination claim.

Victimization   As in the sex discrimination section, an individual can bring a race discrimination case if they have been victimized because they have:

- given evidence or information under, or with reference to, the act
- brought proceedings under the act
- alleged unlawful behaviour on the part of someone else under the act

If an individual alleges race discrimination which subsequently turns out to be untrue, he or she is still protected from victimization, but no if the allegation was made in bad faith.

Interviewing

A prospective employee has grounds for claiming discrimination if there is unfairness in:

1   the arrangements which employers make for deciding who should be offered employment;

2　the terms on which employment is offered;
3　the refusal or deliberate omission to offer employment.

So while the selection interview may only be part of the selecion process, it has an important part to play in ensuring fair, non-discriminatory selection. One recent case pursued by the Commission for Racial Equality (CRE) illustrates this point well. In 1989 the CRE began investigations into the selection and promotion procedures of London Underground Limited (LUL), with, it should be noted, the full cooperation of LUL. This organization used both tests of ability and personality, and panel interviews to reach decisions over internal promotions into newly-created management positions. Not only did the CRE find that the ability tests were unfairly discriminating against Asian and Afro-Caribbean applicants (both groups scored lower than whites), but also that the panel interview was discriminatory, particularly against Asian applicants. LUL responded well to the Commission's findings by suspending the testing procedure and by instituting a full ethnic monitoring system (see later in this chapter for details) and training provisions for their recruitment staff.

This case illustrates that fairness must run all the way through from preparing the person specification (see chapter 2), to making the offer, or declining to do so. In the case of the person specification, the criteria must be both objective and fair. Decisions must not be reached in a subjective or arbitrary way. The courts are becoming increasingly critical of selection practices where there is a lack of a specified, objective, measurable and well-defined criteria. Once criteria have been decided upon, the best candidate according to those criteria should be selected.

In particular, questions asked at interview should studiously avoid remarks or inferences which might give grounds for offence or charges of discrimination. Regrettably, there is still anecdotal evidence of occasional racist questions in interviews. The following is a list of some that the authors have heard about. These, and questions like them, have no place in selection interviews.

Do you intend to return to the West Indies (Pakistan, India, Ireland, etc.)?
What problems do you think you might find from members of the public?
　(Implication: because you are black)
Do you think you'll be able to fit in with white colleagues?
Why do you call yourself British, with an accent like that? (An awful question, but it has been asked)

Would you, like so many other Indians I have employed in the past, keep
wanting long holidays to go back to India?

Do you think our white employees would resent having a black boss?

Being Irish, are you going to lose your temper if annoyed with your fellow
workers?

We like our employees to look smart. Do you have to wear a turban and a
beard?

Most of our Pakistani workers are manual workers. What special qualities
do you have to be considered for this manager's job?

What makes you believe that this company will hire any more coloured
people?

From *How to Pick People for Jobs*, Viv Shackleton (Fontana, 1989).

Questions like these are almost certain to be considered as
treating a candidate less favourably then others on the basis of their
race, colour, nationality or ethnic origins. If a job applicant claims
discrimination on the basis of arrangements made for deciding who
to employ (see above), remarks made at interview can often be very
relevant. An example is *Virdee v ECC Quarry Ltd (1978)*. Mr Virdee
was an Asian who was asked at interview whether he had worked
with white people before and whether he had had any trouble supervising them. This was considered crucial evidence that he had been
discriminated against on account of his race.

As we pointed out in chapter 6, it is good practice always to make
notes during the interview. This is not just to assist the interviewer
to reach a decision on each candidate once they have all been seen,
interview notes can be a valuable source of evidence in a discrimination case. They should be kept for at least six months to
provide supporting evidence that the decision was made according
to the specified objective criteria and not on racial grounds. The
same goes for the results of any other assessment technique such
as test scores or assessment centre ratings. Reasons for refusing
employment to particular candidates should be noted. And, of
course, these principles apply to all interviews, not just to those with
minority group applicants.

Permitted race discrimination

Job quotas which favour one racial group, as well as other forms of
'positive discrimination', are not lawful under the RRA. As with sex
discrimination, there are just a few clearly defined and limited areas
where positive discrimination is permitted. These mostly relate to

training and include special language courses or skills training for racial groups.

In addition, like the SDA, where there is a Genuine Occupational Qualification it is lawful to discriminate. This is where there is a genuine need for the person to be of a certain racial group. There are defined categories of jobs where GOQs can apply and these are:

- Participation in a dramatic performance or other entertainment, where being of a certain racial group is required for authenticity (e.g., a black man playing the part of Othello).
- Participation as a model in a production of a work of art or visual image (e.g., TV), where again a member of a certain racial group is required for authenticity.
- Working in a place where food or drink is provided and consumed by members of the public, where being of a certain racial group is required for authenticity (e.g., a Chinese waiter in a Chinese restaurant).
- A personal provision of welfare services for a particular racial group, where these services can best be provided by someone of the same racial group.

Ethnic monitoring

The Commission for Racial Equality (CRE) in its Code of Practice (1984) strongly recommends monitoring. Employers should keep records of the progress of different racial groups in the workforce and monitor the effects of selection decisions and personnel practices and procedures. The reasons for decisions should be noted. The CRE also recommends that monitoring should be by each plant, department, section, shift and job category, and changes monitored over periods of time.

Figure 8.1 gives examples of monitoring forms designed by the CRE.

There are a number of reasons why monitoring (including sex monitoring) should take place. There are:

1 Morally, as well as legally, employers have a duty to see that employees of whatever race (or either sex) are treated fairly. The only sure way of knowing that personnel practices are not unlawfully discriminating is to keep records. In particular, it allows employers to note the proportion of a minority group who attain higher levels in the organization.

2   If ethnic monitoring shows up patterns of discrimination, it demon-
    strates to employers where matters must be put right. It indicates
    where and in what ways discrimination is taking place and where
    action is needed.
3   A third reason is to enable employers to provide factual, written
    evidence of fair employment practices in the event of a discrimination
    case. Courts take a dim view where discrimination cases are brought
    and ethnic monitoring is absent.

Moreover, the case of *West Midlands Passenger Transport Executive
v Singh (1988)*, shows that courts have wide powers to order the
disclosure of relevant information. Mr Singh, an Asian, was a bus
inspector and had worked for the company for a number of years. In
1985 the bus company with whom he was employed drew up a
shortlist of twenty-six people for the job of senior inspector. Mr
Singh and three other Black inspectors made it onto the shortlist.
Nine inspectors were promoted, all of whom were white. Mr Singh,
supported by the Commission for Racial Equality, claimed racial
discrimination. The company had been monitoring manual jobs,
including that of inspector, for over a year and so was able to
provide full details of the candidates. However, at the industrial
tribunal the company was ordered to produce additional statistics
including details of the ethnic origin of people who had applied for,
or been appointed to, posts within grades similar to that of senior
inspector. The company objected and lost the case. The Court of
Appeal later rejected the employer's appeal.

So industrial tribunals have wide powers and can order disclosure
of monitoring information. The information requested by Mr Singh
and the courts was relevant because it might show that his racial
group had been subject to discrimination. If it did, then the tribunal
could infer that the company had discriminated against Mr Singh.

Other minority groups

In the USA it is also against the law to discriminate on grounds
of age or handicap. This is not the case in Britain. However, even
though there is no law against it, responsible employers still have
a duty to interview and select fairly. Ethical interviews are those
where all the questions can be shown to have a relationship to job
requirements. If only fair and relevant questions are asked, the

Form A: Distribution of employees by ethnic group

Industrial employees section .... Date ....

	BLACK				WHITE		
Origin:	Afro-Caribbean	African	Asian	Other	European (including UK)	Other	TOTAL
Maintenance engineers							
Production workers:							
Grade A							
B							
C							
D							
E							
Despatch							
Chargehands							
Supervisors							

Industrial employees section .... Date ....

	BLACK				WHITE		
Origin:	Afro-Caribbean	African	Asian	Other	European (including UK)	Other	TOTAL
Typists							
Secretaries							
Clerical staff:							
Grade: A							
B							
C							
Supervisory							
Managerial							
Technical							
Professional							

Form B: Recruitment records

Date of application	Name/Address of applicant	Ethnic origins	Post applied for	Result of application	Reason for rejection (where appropriate)

Note: A similar form might be used for applications for internal upgrading, training, promotion, etc.

Figure 8.1 Monitoring forms.

Form C: Analysis of recruitment statistics Period from .... to ....

		BLACK				WHITE		
		Afro-Caribbean origin	African origin	Asian origin	Other	European origin (including UK)	Other	TOTAL
	(a) (b)	Number applied/ engaged	Number applied/ engaged	Number applied/ engaged	Number applied/ engaged	Number applied/ engaged	Number applied/ engaged	Number applied/ engaged
Industrial employees								
Maintenance	(a) (b)							
Production (according to grade)	(a) (b)							
Despatch	(a) (b)							
Supervisory	(a) (b)							
TOTAL	(a) (b)							

Note: A similar report/summary form might be used for internal upgrading, training, promotion, etc.

Figure 8.1 *(cont.)*

interview should have no adverse impact on minorities. Unfortunately, anecdotal evidence suggests that this is often not the case. Even if unfair questions are avoided, interviewers' questions can often convey an impression of discriminatory intent.

In addition, it is likely that unfair discrimination takes place before the interview stage. One study in Britain (Brown and Gay, 1985) showed that ethnic applicants matched in terms of gender, experience and qualifications were less successful in being *called for* interview in three major UK cities. The same is probably true for the disabled and older age groups. One notorious fact is that many jobs are advertised with age restrictions (such as 'should ideally be under 45') which seem very hard to justify in objective, job-related terms, and are against the recommendations of the IPM Recruitment Code (1991).

Finally, other minority groups not covered by law even in the USA, such as gay men and lesbians and candidates who have AIDS, may well be discriminated against, even though at the moment there are virtually no verifiable, documented examples. All one can hope is that books such as these will encourage interviewers to select only on grounds of suitability for the job, and avoid unethical and unfairly discriminatory questions or decisions.

Concluding Comments

Discrimination is a sensitive issue. But this is no excuse for not considering it openly and carefully when interviewing. It is the interviewer's responsibility to select fairly and to give not the slightest cause for complaint. Although the legislation is not as strict, nor the penalties for non-compliance as severe, in Britain as it is in the USA, it goes without saying that it should be upheld. Industrial tribunal awards can be considerable, and the potential damage to a reputation severe, if an organization is found to have contravened the law. More importantly, discrimination has no part in the modern organization in Britain.

On a final note, you will find a light-hearted equal opportunities law quiz in the following pages. Hopefully it will stimulate your thoughts on the avoidance of discrimination. Although it is not a validated instrument, in addition it might give you an indication of how much you have learned in this chapter. Since we are about to turn to the question of training and developing interviewers, it serves as an introduction to the important topic of the evaluation of training and development activities.

DISCRIMINATION LAW QUIZ

Instructions

For each of the questions below, see if you think it is unlawful discrimination or not. If you think it is unlawful, try to decide whether it is direct or indirect discrimination. Answers are on page 170.

Sex discrimination questions

1   Ms G and another woman were appointed to two jobs which involved working with men. The other woman failed to turn up for the work. In the past there had been problems with one woman working with an all-male team, so the company decided that it was in Mrs G's best interests that she should not be allowed to start work.
    Unlawful discrimination? YES/NO
    direct/indirect discrimination
2   A female applicant was not offered a job in a mens' clothes shop on the grounds that she would have to take inside leg measurements.

Unlawful discrimination? YES/NO
direct/indirect discrimination

3 A woman was promoted on condition that she taught badminton after school. After leave of absence to adopt a child, she refused to undertake after-school coaching and was demoted.
Unlawful discrimination? YES/NO
direct/indirect discrimination

4 A single parent asked to transfer from full-time to part-time employment to enable her to look after her two dependant children. This was refused by the employer. The employer required the job to be held by a full-timer.
Unlawful discrimination? YES/NO
direct/indirect discrimination

5 An applicant applied for a job in a travel agency. During the course of the interview he mentioned that his wife worked for a rival firm. He was not appointed because it was felt that there would be a risk of loss of confidentiality which would be detrimental for business.
Unlawful discrimination? YES/NO
direct/indirect discrimination

6 An applicant, a single man, applied for a job as a commercial traveller. He was rejected in favour of a married man because the employer felt that married men offer more stability.
Unlawful discrimination? YES/NO
direct/indirect discrimination

Race discrimination questions

1 A candidate was not considered a suitable applicant for a job with a Welsh county council on the grounds of not being a Welsh speaker.
Unlawful discrimination? YES/NO
direct/indirect discrimination

2 A London borough advertised for posts of group manager and assistant head of housing benefits. The advertisement stipulated that because the services were to be provided to the black community, only Afro-Caribbean and Asian applicants should apply.
Unlawful discrimination? YES/NO
direct/indirect discrimination

3 An applicant applied for a job but wasn't considered because he lived in Liverpool 8. The employers had made a requirement that applicants who lived in certain Liverpool postal districts would

not be considered. The specified districts had a high proportion of non-white residents. The candidate lived in one of those districts.
Unlawful discrimination? YES/NO
direct/indirect discrimination

4   A Rastafarian was refused a job as a van driver because he would not cut his dreadlocks.
Unlawful discrimination? YES/NO
direct/indirect discrimination

5   A female applicant of black African origin applied for a job with a firm whose main customer was a South African company. The job would involve contact with visiting South African representatives visiting the firm. She was not offered the job because it was felt that the visitors might object to her being black.
Unlawful discrimination? YES/NO
direct/indirect discrimination

6   An Indian candidate applied for a job as a chef in a Thai restaurant. He was refused on the grounds that only people of Thai origin were employed in the restaurant to preserve its authenticity.
Unlawful discrimination? YES/NO
direct/indirect discrimination

Answers

Sex discrimination

1   YES, it is direct discrimination. Although done with the best of intentions, the motive of the employer is irrelevant.
Grieg v Community Industry (1979)

2   YES, it is direct discrimination. The employer contended that it was a GOQ (a 'Genuine Occupational Qualification') to have a man to undertake this duty in order to preserve decency and privacy. This was not accepted by the tribunal because there were seven male assistants who could undertake this task when necessary. An employer should attempt to redistribute the 'single-sex' duties if it is reasonable to do so, and there are sufficient staffing levels for this to be done without undue inconvenience. Only if this redistribution is not possible can an employer attempt to claim a GOQ.
Wylie v Dee & Co (Menswear) Ltd (1978)

3   NO, this was not judged to be discrimination. The Court of Appeal did hold that the requirement was one with which a smaller

proportion of women than men could comply. But by applying a test of justifiability, it found that it was reasonable in the interests of the school that coaching should take place after school. Therefore the discriminatory effect was justified and not unlawful.
Briggs v North Eastern Education and Library Board (1990)

4　YES, this was indirect discrimination because it had a disproportionate effect in respect of women with children. The employer was not able to show that it was a justifiable requirement that the work should only be organized on a full-time basis.
Home Office v Holmes (1984)

5　NO, because the risk involved for the business would have applied equally if the applicant were a woman. Therefore there was no discrimination on the grounds of sex. It would also have applied to a non-married couple of close association and therefore there was no marriage discrimination either.

6　NO, single people are not covered by the marital status section of the SDA. If the applicant had been married and rejected because the employer liked commercial travellers to be single, then this would be discrimination on the grounds of marital status.

Race discrimination

1　NO, this is not unlawful indirect discrimination because race is not defined by the characteristic of language alone. Although it was accepted that being Welsh is to belong to a distinct ethnic group, there is no racial group of English-speaking Welsh. So a condition requiring that applicants must be able to speak Welsh cannot constitute unlawful discrimination on the grounds of race.
Gwynedd CC v Jones (1986)

2　YES, direct discrimination. This is not a case of GOQ. The posts were managerial and administrative and so involved little contact with the public. They could not be classified as providing a *personal* service to any member of a racial group and therefore this was not a GOQ.
London Borough of Lambeth v CRE (1990)

3　YES, this was found to be indirect discrimination. Fifty per cent of the population in the specified districts were non-white as compared with the rest of Merseyside where the figure was about two per cent. Therefore, certain racial groups were disproportionately affected.
Hussein v Saints Complete House Furnitures (1979)

4　NO, for similar reasons to question 1 in this section, but only after appeal. The tribunal ruled that this was unlawful indirect discrimination on the grounds that Rastafarians were a racial group. However, the EAT (Employment Appeal Tribunal) upheld the employer's appeal because it was doubtful whether Rastafarians could claim a group descent or group history. There was not enough to distinguish them from the rest of the Afro-Caribbean community so as to render them a separate group. *Crown Suppliers (PSA) v Dawkins (1991)*

5   YES, this is direct discrimination. Employers cannot justify discrimination on the grounds that customers or employees are prejudiced, even if they can prove that they will lose business as a result.

6   YES, because he would be working in the kitchen and not seen by customers. Therefore, the claim of GOQ is not justified. If he had applied for a job as a waiter, it would have been a different matter.

Summary Propositions

1   The Sex Discrimination Act and the Race Relations Act are designed to help eliminate discrimination in employment. They prohibit discrimination:
    (a)   in the arrangements made to decide who will be offered employment;
    (b)   in the employment terms offered;
    (c)   by refusing or deliberately omitting to offer that person employment.

2   The IPM, EOC, CRE, and BPS publish codes of practice covering fair selection.

3   Under the acts, there are three ways an employer can discriminate. These are:
    (a)   direct discrimination;
    (b)   indirect discrimination;
    (c)   victimization.
    It is also illegal to discriminate on grounds of marital status.

4   Each of the acts permits discrimination where there is a Genuine Occupational Qualification, but such cases are limited in number and carefully defined.

5   Ethnic monitoring by employers is strongly recommended by the Commission for Racial Equality, and is most definitely good practice.

6   Other forms of discrimination, such as on the grounds of age or disability, are not currently prohibited by law, but are against the IPM Code of Practice, as well as those of other institutions.

References

Bowers, J. (1990) *Employment Law* (London: Blackstone Press Limited).

British Psychological Society (1980) *Discriminating Fairly: A Guide to Fair Selection* (London: The Runnymead Trust and The British Psychological Society).

Brown, E. and Gay, P. (1985) *Racial Discrimination 17 Years after the Act* Policy Studies Institute, No. 646, London.

Commission for Racial Equality (1984) *Code of Practice, The Elimination of Race Discrimination in Employment* (London: HMSO).

Equal Opportunities Commission (1985) *Code of Practice on Sex Discrimination* (London: HMSO).

Institute of Personnel Management (1990) *The IPM Equal Opportunities Code* (London: IPM).

Institute of Personnel Management (1991) *Recruitment Code* (London: IPM).

Lewis, D. (1990) *Essentials of Employment Law* (third Edition) (London: IPM).

Selwyn, N. M. (1988) *Law of Employment* (sixth Edition) (London: Butterworths).

Younson, F. (1987) *Employment Law Handbook* (Aldershot, Hants: Gower).

9

Training and Developing the Interviewer

'Literally thousands of practising managers have said that they learned to interview through trial and error, with no instruction or coaching. . . . many are simply told that they have staffing responsibilities and will need to interview applicants.'

Goodale, *Effective Employment Interviewing*, 1989

Almost every candidate for a job in Britain is interviewed (Shackleton and Newell, 1991). Some of them may find other methods, such as tests, being used as well but all will be subjected to the interview. This places a great deal of importance on the selector being good at the task of interviewing.

Personnel professionals have often been through courses, such as those leading to IPM qualifications, which take interviewing skills seriously. They know (or should know) the correct methods, the potential pitfalls, and be practised in conducting effective interviews. Yet many day-to-day interviews are conducted by managers or professionals who are not human resource specialists. They may be engineers, accountants, teachers or police officers who have interviewing tacked on to their 'regular' job. They have not been through courses which examine the skills and knowledge behind selection interviewing. Interviewing is something they do infrequently and sometimes without any training at all. It is not surprising, then, that the research evidence reviewed in chapter 3 suggests that the usual, unstructured selection interview has poor predictive validity.

Worse, some managers and professionals assume that they do not need interviewer training. They think they are good at interviewing. They may recognize that others could do with some improvement, but not them. There is a commonly quoted saying that there are only three things everybody believes they are good at – driving a car, making love, and interviewing. Yet all of these activities can benefit from practice and experience, but only if people are prepared to admit that their technique is not perfect. At least, not yet.

Employers are very ill-advised to assume that otherwise effective employees are capable of conducting good interviews. Yet the importance of interviewing cannot be overstated. Recruitment is expensive and appointing an ineffective candidate a very costly mistake (see chapter 1). Even those rejected need to feel well treated. To take just one example, 'milk-round' (campus recruitment) interviewers convey an impression of their company to undergraduates. Clumsy, arrogant, or uninterested interviewers do themselves and their company no good. Research has shown that one of the major factors in a student's decision to reject or keep alive their application to a company is the way they are treated by the milk-round interviewer (Keenan and Wedderburn, 1980). And the students' grapevine is very powerful. Students listen to, and place credence on, what other students say. Negative impressions of companies spread far and fast.

Training Needs

All of the above argues for interviewers to be trained. Any training and development process should move from an assessment of need, through the development of the programme, to evaluation of what has been achieved.

So what specific knowledge and skill do interviewers need? What are the common pitfalls for the inexperienced? What problems do even experienced interviewers have that training might address? A book concerned with interviewer training and published by the IPM (Hackett, 1990) lists a number of pitfalls for the inexperienced:

- lack of clarity about the objectives of the interview
- failure to work out which topics are likely to elicit most useful information
- failure to structure the interview properly
- failure to provide the right physical setting
- failure to ask the right questions, in the right way
- talking too much
- not listening
- jumping to conclusions

- failure to probe, especially in what look like areas of weakness
- low recall of information
- bias or prejudice in evaluation
- a tendency to try and assess the interviewee as a whole rather than building up a picture systematically
- concentration on personality traits rather than results and behaviour
- lack of effective follow-up.

Similarly, a research-based book lists seven areas which even experienced interviewers mention as problems (Goodale, 1989):

1 uncertainty about the information they need to gather and how to ask questions to get it
2 not knowing how to get information without violating equal opportunities guidelines
3 their own personal attitudes and stereotypes, first-impression biases, and early decisions
4 quiet, evasive and polished applicants
5 lack of skill in breaking through the applicant's facade and prepared answers
6 not knowing how to evaluate what the applicant says
7 not knowing how to make the hiring decision

To avoid the pitfalls and to deal with the problems outlined above, training is required. There are two main parts to the training – knowledge and skill. These have been referred to earlier in the book as, respectively, the cognitive and social skills aspects of interviewing. The knowledge or theoretical aspects can be gained by reading or by lecture. But the skill aspects are best acquired by doing. In the training context this is by supervised practice. So the three main components of a training programme are:

- theory and knowledge acquisition;
- supervised skill practice;
- critical but constructive feedback on skill acquisition.

Principles of effective training

Once it has been decided what trainees need to learn, it is possible to design the interview training programme. There are several methods and types of training, which we will describe shortly, but each aims to help trainees perform at a desired level of proficiency.

There are some well accepted principles which help make any training effective. Any professionally designed course will embody some or all of these principles. Four of the major principles are:

- *Participation* helps trainees learn quicker and more effectively. So a training programme should encourage participation by discussion groups, role plays, exercises and skill practice.
- *Repetition* of the desired behaviour improves learning. So an interviewing programme should be designed to encourage practice of the new skills on more than one occasion, perhaps using different methods. Actual interviewing 'for real' shortly after the course, along with feedback, helps ensure that the skill is practised again. There is the story of the golf professional who was congratulated on his luck at winning the tournament, to which he replied : 'Yet, it's strange. The more I practise the luckier I get.'
- *Transference* of training is the extent to which the learning achieved on the programme is transferred to the job. After all, it is effective job performance that is the goal. The simple principle is: the closer the programme matches the job, the better the transference. That is why well designed interview programmes use simulations, role plays and, best of all, what we refer to later in this chapter as 'real life interviews'.
- *Feedback* is letting participants know what they are doing well and not well. It is a point we will refer to constantly in this chapter. Without knowledge of results, little skill is acquired. Imagine for a moment someone typing this chapter on a word processor. Say that person is a fairly poor typist but getting better. Without the feedback he or she receives every minute, from seeing the correct or incorrect letters appear on the screen, how will that person ever get proficient? In the context of interview training, great skill at feedback is needed on the part of the tutor to get participants to see their mistakes and improve. Yet without effective feedback, little learning takes place.

Types of training programme: Off-the-peg or tailor-made?

There is a vast array of commercially available, *off-the-peg*, courses which deal with all aspects of recruitment including interviewing. They are frequently advertised in personnel management and training publications as well as in other professional literature. These are 'open' courses or seminars, in the sense that they are open to people from all types of organization, manufacturing or service, public sector or private, commercial or not-for-profit, large or small. They are off-the-peg and neither require nor offer any customization for a particular customer.

There are several major advantages to such courses. They tend to be less expensive than tailor-made though, with accommodation charges as well as fees, rarely cheap. They provide the advantage to course participants of being able to compare their own company methods and procedures with those of other organizations. This might be done formally, during sessions, or informally outside normal session hours, such as in the bar or over dinner. The courses are often well designed, professionally presented and achieve favourable ratings from participants.

The disadvantages are that the timing of such programmes may be inconvenient, they work out very expensive if more than one or two delegates from one organization attend and, most importantly they cater for a mass audience. So they are unlikely to address specific company problems, practices or procedures. They will not use case studies or examples directly related to one particular organization – the delegate's own. Delegates may well have some difficulty transferring the general knowledge and skill gained to the specific application in their own organization.

Tailor-made courses, seminars or workshops aim to customize interview training to a client's organization. They will use case studies or practical examples drawn from that organization. Where practice interviews are part of the training, the usual in-company application forms, scoring sheets or test package can be incorporated. 'Guinea pig' candidates for interview role plays can be similar to real candidates with which delegates are, or will later become, familiar. If there is a series of these courses, then modifications to the design are more easily incorporated if post-course evaluation suggests that they are needed.

A major disadvantage is cost. Development and design of such a programme can involve anything from a day to two person/weeks, depending on the number of specially designed exercises. However, where there is a large number of delegates such development costs are spread thinly and tailor-made may well mean cost-effective. The other potential disadvantage lies in the choice of course director and presenter. If in-house personnel are used to conduct the programme, they may not be such polished course delivery professionals as the open programme presenter who is "on the boards" in front of an audience scores of weeks a year. On the other hand, if outside consultants are used, they may be experts at selection and effective presenters, but some of the in-house knowledge of specific selection methods is inevitably lost. The best solution is often a course which combines both specialists. The lead tutor is an external consultant with specialist expertise, supported by an internal HRM professional with knowledge of the organization's selection systems and practice.

Training methods

As we stated earlier, the aim of the training programme is to develop knowledge and skills in interviewing. This leaves the choice of methods wide open.

The primary need is to provide opportunities for the trainees to practise and receive feedback on the necessary skills. This implies an emphasis on the 'doing' under supervised instruction, rather than formal, non-participative, instructional methods. It implies lots of practice trials so that improvements can be made and the learning reinforced. Finally, it implies constructive criticism. This helps the participant to recognize errors, know why they occurred, and consider ways of eradicating them. It also means trainees are helped to recognize when they have done something right so that this effective use of skill is encouraged.

However, practice without knowledge and thought about what should be achieved is sterile. An effective programme needs to start with knowledge. It needs to encourage trainees to assess what interviewing aims ot achieve and what skills are required to accomplish these aims. Methods for this part of the programme are likely to be rather more static and formal.

In the sections which follow, we describe a number of possible methods. No one technique is necessarily better than another. They all have strengths and weaknesses. But some may be better at achieving one objective rather than another. In practice, a range of methods is likely to be found in any particular training event. Here we group methods into three broad categories, lectures and video, discussions, and exercises.

1 Lectures and videos Lectures and commercially available videos or films provide information. They can help participants understand the importance of job analysis and person specifications, introduce theoretical models, point to the purpose of interviewing, examine good practice, and illustrate some of the problems and pitfalls. In fact, in a brief way, they can cover the contents of this book so far. In addition, films or videos can show 'model' or ideal behaviour that trainees should attempt to copy. Recent research has shown this modelling can be an effective training method (Decker and Nathan, 1985).

However, it is not possible to lay down many prescriptive rules for effective interviewing. While errors can be highlighted, effective interviewing is more difficult to define. Exactly the 'right' questions can be asked, but the answers may go unregistered by the interviewer. On the other hand, useful outcomes can be achieved by interested and empathic interviewers, even if their questioning technique is poor (see chapters 6 and 7).

Often all lectures and videos really do is raise awareness. They cannot help trainees to develop their interview techniques. They cannot cover all aspects of selection interviewing. They cannot ensure that the information is understood or remembered. And they cannot please everyone all the time. One particular lecture or video style may appeal to one delegate and not another. Take the example of humour. To some, a presenter's bouncy, humorous, jocular style may be just the thing to enthuse, amuse and motivate the delegate to think and learn. To others in the audience it may seem flip, irrelevant, irritating or downright offensive. Without discussion, lectures and videos are limited to talking about principles of good practice and the theoretical models that lie behind these principles.

2 Discussions Lectures and videos are much more effective if participants are encouraged to actively participate in discussions. These can take place during the information input or in smaller 'breakout' groups afterwards. They serve the purpose of clarifying understanding, challenging previously held assumptions and attitudes, and focusing attention on the major learning points. Breakout groups, in particular, can be used to encourage delegates to compare views frankly with one another, understand or challenge each others' attitudes, help retention of information by designing checklists or making presentations, and building commitment to the learning process.

Discussions on their own, though, cannot develop interview techniques or ensure that the learning is retained. Unless they are focused with clear objectives and properly managed they will be seen as frustratingly irrelevant by participants.

3 Exercises Four types of exercise can be considered. They are:

(a) ice-breakers
(b) case studies
(c) role plays
(d) real-life interviews

For the last two methods in this list, the addition of closed circuit television (CCTV) and constructive feedback add immeasurably to their effectiveness, and we will discuss these two issues separately.

(a) *Ice-breaker exercises* Ice-breakers are short exercises that are used at the beginning of programmes to relax delegates and to help them get to know each other. In interview training modules they can also be used to provide practice in questioning techniques. Instead of the usual ice-breaker of 'spend two minutes introducing yourself to the rest of the group', delegates can be asked to introduce *another* course member. The trainer pairs up delegates and allows five or ten minutes aside for them to interview each other. At the end of this time delegates introduce their partner to the rest of the group. Missed information, inaccurate recall or observations on questioning techniques can be discussed. However, ice-breaker exercises can lend themselves to the criticism of 'time-wasting little games' and need to be seen as relevant to the course as a whole, and well managed by the tutor, to be effective.

(b) *Case study exercises* Case studies are a popular vehicle for learning on courses. They tend to be paper-based exercises and describe a scenario (real or imaginary) about which delegates make decisions and later discuss with fellow course members and tutors. They can range from short descriptions of candidates to longer cases which take delegates through the major steps in the selection process as a whole. This book (as well as others (Goodworth, 1979; Shackleton, 1989)) contains examples of such cases. Case study exercises are another useful way of helping delegates to think about the interviewing or selection process before tackling the practical skills involved. The discussion phase can expose entrenched attitudes or blinkered thinking which are then more amenable to challenge and change. Their limitations are, as with any exercise, that they can be dismissed as artificial, too much like games, and divorced from the real world. They do not help participants acquire the interpersonal skills they need for interviews. But they can improve the evidence weighing and decision making aspects of interviewing.

(c) *Role play exercises* Role plays are a very popular method of acquiring interviewing skills and can be divided into unbriefed or briefed role plays. In unbriefed, or spontaneous, role play the trainee reacts to the situation presented and is given no briefing or guidelines. With briefed role play trainees are provided with briefs which describe the person and the situation and which guide their actions. Briefed role play is not the same as acting. The briefs guide rather than provide a script. The role player invents questions, responses and statements which are in character and mirror the situation, but they are not overly constrained in what they say. After each role play comes analysis and discussion where critical evaluation takes place.

Unbriefed role play has only a limited part to play in selection interviewing, although it is used a great deal in other forms of interview and social skills training, such as assertiveness training, counselling, and grievance interviews. In selection interview training, mini-role plays involving selector and interviewee are used to practise questioning techniques, such as the use of open and closed questions, or summarizing and reflecting back (see chapter 6).

Briefed role plays are more common. They might be tailor-made or off-the-shelf. They help improve the skills of questioning and collecting relevant information upon which to make a decision. The fact that data is provided in the brief means that there is an objective way of assessing how much of the relevant information has been obtained. A role play is the only method discussed up to now which allows a complete interview to be undertaken, involving preparation, planning, performance and review. It gives delegates the chance to see what it feels like to be an interviewer. It also gives interviewee role players a glimpse of what it feels like to be a candidate, which helps empathy when that person is interviewing for real.

The drawback to either type of role play is that they often feel like play acting. Role-playing a candidate who is very different from oneself in age, background, qualifications or experience is difficult. That feeling of difficulty is transmitted to the interviewer, who finds choosing questions or evaluating answers doubly difficult as a consequence. In addition, tutors often find that trainees want to analyse the *content* of the interview ('She had no degree, did you spot that?' or 'He seemed very keen on football') rather than the *process* of questioning, probing, finding out a track record, relating previous job experience to the job on offer, and so on.

(d) *Using 'real-life' interviews*   Probably the best method of training interview skills is to use real-life interviewees. These are people who want to be interviewed, who are qualified for the jobs available and who mirror very closely a typical candidate. Such people are not too hard to find. Graduate recruiters will find a ready supply of willing interviewees by contacting a local university. Recruiters of school leavers can approach the headteacher of a local school and request some of their keen sixth formers or final year pupils to act as interview guinea pigs. One of the authors recently helped train panel interviewers for a county police force 'Special Constables' who wanted to join the regular force, or who had recently been turned down and asked to reapply later, were only too pleased to help. The common denominator is choosing people who want to gain interview practice and are qualified for the posts. Most job seekers welcome the chance to improve their self-presentation skills and will be quite willing to participate in return for feedback on their performance.

The logistics and sequencing of these real-life interviews are as follows. Candidates receive a job description and complete an application form which is available to the interviewers before the interview. Trainees are divided into small groups and take turns to interview candidates or observe the interview. Candidates can be interviewed more than once by separate groups of delegates. Candidates comment on the interview from the interviewee's perspective and receive feedback from the observer group, the interviewer, the course director, or all three. This should of course be handled sensitively. It is often best to arrange private feedback for the candidate. The interviewee is thanked, paid (hopefully!) and departs. On some occasions, candidates stay and assist the full debrief but this can mean that interviewers become too defensive and learning is handicapped. Finally, the full debrief of the interview takes place, guided by the tutor, and the learning points summarized.

The obvious advantage of using real job seekers is that the credibility of the exercise is high, which aids learning. If the interview lasts long enough (around twenty-thirty minutes) and if the time allowed for post-interview discussion is ample, using real-life interviewees is a powerful learning vehicle.

The limitations are that it takes more administrative setting-up time than using delegates as role play interviewees. If the outside candidates do not possess the relevant qualifications or experience for the job on offer, it is advisable to use delegates as interviewees, since they are likely to want to help create a useful learning experience for their colleagues. Outside guinea pig interviewees are usually more interested in their own learning!

(e)   *Closed circuit television*   Earlier in this chapter we laid emphasis on the importance of constructive feedback as an essential element in the skill training process. Closed circuit television (CCTV) can be of enormous help. It is best arranged such that the interview takes place in one room and the observers watch on a monitor in another. That way both interviewer and interviewee avoid the distractions of laughter, rustling of paper, conversations between observers and the general intrusive presence of others. Recordings of the interview allow the participant to see themselves conducting the interview once it is over. They hear and see exactly what was said and done. Questioning techniques, body posture, facial expressions, and time management, can all be analysed in the most minute detail if required. Watching the recording afterwards can focus the discussion, reminding observers of their observations and can even be given to the interviewer to study in his or her own time. This opportunity to watch in relative peace and quiet is particularly useful for the nervous interviewer, for whom the interview itself probably passed by in a daze.

The only limitation is that reviewing the interview can take enormous amounts of time. A half-hour interview can easily take three times as long to debrief with the aid of the recording. But it is this feedback which is of major benefit, as we have said before. Time should be made available to exploit the medium for the learning it can bring about.

(f)   *Peer feedback*   Although it is the course tutor who has prime responsibility for managing the feedback session, the delegates themselves can have an important role to play in giving feedback to each other. It is often a good idea to give delegates a specific role as observer as well as interviewer. The observer's responsibility could be to focus on one particular interviewer and pick out, say, two examples of good interview practice, and two examples of areas for improvement. The onus is on the tutor to insist that positive as well as negative feedback is given. Observing and commenting on the performance of others is almost as valuable a learning experience as receiving feedback. Adopting this technique has the added advantage of involving delegates throughout the *whole* process and not just when interviewing. If they know that they are going to give feedback, they are less likely to go to sleep while watching others perform!

The following is a sample outline of a two-day training programme which incorporates the topics and methods discussed above. This is one suggestion based on training programmes designed by the authors. It could easily be adapted to suit the needs of other trainers.

A sample two-day training course

Day 1

9.00   Topic: Introductions.
          Method: Ice-breaker.

9.15   Topic: The process of selection and the skills of interviewing.
          Method: Talk and discussion.

10.30   Coffee.

10.45   Topic: Designing person specification from job descriptions based on a 'target' job in the organization and descriptions provided by personnel department. Criteria for selection.
          Method: Practical work in small groups. Small group presentation at plenary session with tutor-guided feedback.

12.00   Topic: Questioning techniques.
          Method: Talk, discussion and role play.

1.00   Lunch.

2.00   Topic: Studying real-life candidates' application forms in preparation for practical interviewing sessions. Deciding on areas to be probed and types of questions to be asked.
          Method: Individual preparation followed by small group work, guided by tutor.

3.00   Topic: One-to-one interviewing of real-life candidates.
          Method: Small groups with interviews recorded on CCTV and group feedback aided by tutor.

5.30   Close.

Day 2

9.00	Topic:	Good and not-so-good interviews.
	Method:	Video of interview methods followed by discussion.
10.30		Coffee.
10.45	Topic:	More about skills of interviewing, including note-taking, non-verbal communication, rapport building and closing the interview.
	Method:	Talk, discussion and role play.
12.00	Topic:	Study and discussion of application forms for afternoon session.
	Method:	Individual preparation and small group work.
1.00		Lunch.
2.00	Topic:	One-to-one interviews of real-life candidates.
	Method:	CCTV and group feedback aided by tutor.
5.00		Conclusions, summary of learning points and farewells.
5.30		Close.

Does Training Work?: The Importance of Evaluation

It is important to evaluate any training programme to examine whether it has achieved its aims and objectives and whether modification is needed. Without evaluation, programme designers and tutors have no clear idea of whether the programme is effectively training and developing participants, or is a waste time and money.

In practice most courses are not fully or systematically evaluated. The most that happens is that a short questionnaire is distributed at the end asking participants to rate the course. Cynics call these questionnaires 'happy sheets' because they ask for immediate thoughts and feelings rather than assessing whether learning has occurred. Alternatively, the course tutor or a 'sponsoring manager' (the person paying the bill or the manager sending the delegate on the course) asks orally for some reactions from participants. While it is useful to collect trainees' comments, it is only a small part of a systematic evaluation. There are four main types of data which can be collected (Kirkpatrick, 1967):

- reaction
- learning
- behaviour
- results

Reaction data, such as that described above, is the minimum level of evaluation. While they may be useful, 'happy sheets' may easily give a false picture of the value of the training event. Trainees may give a glowing picture because they laughed a lot and had a good time, but may have learned very little. On the other hand, they may have felt uncomfortable, insecure, had their preconceptions challenged or worked very long hours, and so give poor reports of the programme. Yet they may well have learned a number of new skills. The *value* of training is difficult to assess from reaction data.

Learning data assesses whether trainees have achieved the learning objectives of the programme. One way of doing this is to use written tests before and after the event to check understanding of the material covered. For example, if an objective of part of the interview programme was to familiarize participants with the equal opportunities legislation and codes of practice, a test before and after could assess how much their knowledge and understanding had improved. Although learning data is an improvement on reaction data, it is still limited. It tells course designers whether trainees understand, but it gives no indication of whether they can put this knowledge into practice. They may understand the Sex Discrimination Act, but still find it impossible not to ask discriminatory questions or make decisions which discriminate against women candidates.

Behaviour data is concerned with assessing the impact of the training on behaviour in the workplace. Trainees may show interviewing skill on the course, but can they interview when it really matters, back at work? If not, then favourable evaluations of the course (reaction) and lots of understanding (learning) matter very little. Assessing behaviour change in the workplace is complicated, often involving supervisor or colleague ratings, and beyond the scope of this book. But true programme evaluation should attempt to measure it.

Results orientated evaluation concerns the effect of training on the overall effectiveness (or results) of the organization as a whole. Assuming that a principal aim of training is to improve the success of the organization, the question is: has the training programme

succeeded in its aim? In practice, this question is virtually impossible to answer. This is because so many factors cause organizational
success or failure that it is almost impossible to isolate the effects of
training. For example, one of the authors recently ran a series of
courses for a major public sector employer. These courses centred
around helping senior staff conduct non-discriminatory interviews.
Since that time, there have been no complaints from minority group
candidates and no referrals to industrial tribunals. But is this
success due to the training courses? Who knows? Perhaps it is just
luck. Or perhaps other equal opportunities initiatives by the
organization have raised awareness of this sensitive topic, so that
discrimination has been avoided. On a more obvious level, can a
reduction in labour turnover be attributed to improvements in the
predictive validity of interviews, following a training programme,
or is it a result of the economic climate? Or improved pay and
benefits? Or better industrial relations? Disentangling the results of
training from the myriad of other influences on organizational life
often proves to be impossible.

Despite the problems inherent in measuring the 'bottom line'
results from training, results orientated evaluation should be a long-
term objective. In the meantime, investing in training is often an act
of faith. A recent television programme featured a Ford Motor
Company course on managing change (Business Matters, BBC2, 13
August 1992). The chief executive of Ford stated that despite the
recession and cutbacks in staff and working time, one economy that
would *not* be made was to reduce or scrap this training programme.
It was too important for that. In fact, they were going to be
extending it. Obviously some executives believe that training affects
the success of an organization.

Summary Propositions

1 Training is needed before one can interview effectively.
2 The training process starts with an assessment of training needs. For
   selection interviewing, there is typically a considerable number of
   specific skills which need to be acquired by the interviewer, as well as
   pitfalls for the unwary.
3 Effective training programmes, whether they are provided off-the-peg
   or tailor-made, are based on sound learning principles. These include:
   (a) Participation
   (b) Repetition

    (c)   Transference
    (d)   Feedback
4   There are a variety of possible training methods. These include:
    (a)   Lectures, videos and films
    (b)   Discussion groups
    (c)   Exercises. Some of the popular ones are:
          Ice-breakers
          Case studies
          Role plays
          Real-life interviews
5   The use of CCTV helps participants to watch their own interviewing techniques and learn from feedback. Sensitive, constructive feedback from tutors and fellow participants is invaluable as an aid to learning.
6   No training programme is complete without evaluation to assess whether the aims and objectives of the programme have been achieved. There are four main types of data which can be collected for evaluation purposes. These are:
    (a)   Reaction
    (b)   Learning
    (c)   Behaviour
    (d)   Results

References

Decker, P. J. and Nathan, B. R. (1985) *Behavior Modeling Training* (New York: Praeger).

Goodale, J. G. (1989) Effective Employment Interviewing, in R. W. Eder, and G. R. Ferris, (eds) *The Employment Interview: Theory, Research and Practice* (London: Sage).

Goodworth, C. (1979) *Effective Interviewing* (London: Hutchinson).

Hackett, P. (1990) *Interview Skills Training* (third Edition) (London: Institute of Personnel Management).

Keenan, A. and Wedderburn, A. A. I. (1980) Putting the Boot on the Other Foot: candidates' descriptions of interviews, *Journal of Occupational Psychology*, 53, 81–9.

Kirkpatrick, D. L. (1967) Evaluation of Training, in R. L. Craig and L. R. Bittel (eds) *Training and Development Handbook* (New York: McGraw-Hill).

Shackleton, V. J. (1989) *How to Pick People for Jobs* (London: Fontana).

Shackleton, V. J. and Newell, S. (1991) Management Selection: a comparative study of methods used in top British and French companies, *Journal of Occupational Psychology*, 64, 1, 13–36.

Appendix I
Major Test Suppliers

ASE
Darville House
2 Oxford Road East
Windsor
Berkshire SL4 1DF
Tel 0753 850333

Consulting Psychologists Press Inc.
3803E Bayshore Road
Palo Alto
CA 94303
USA

NFER Nelson
Darville House
2 Oxford Road East
Windsor
Berkshire SL4 1DF
Tel 0753 858961

SRA/London House
9701 West Higgins Road
Rosemont
IL 60018
USA

Oxford Psychologists Press
Lambourne House
311–321 Banbury Road
Oxford OX2 7JH
Tel 0865 510203

Saville & Holdsworth Ltd
3AC Court
High Street
Thames Ditton
Surrey KT7 OSR
Tel 081 398 4170

The Psychological Corporation
Foots Cray High Street
Sidcup
Kent DA14 4BR
Tel 081 300 3322

The Test Agency
Cournswood House
North Dean
High Wycombe
Buckinghamshire HP14 4NW
Tel 024 024 3384

Appendix II
Further Reading

This bibliography is not intended to be an exhaustive review of all texts in print dealing with various aspects of recruitment and selection. Rather, it provides suggestions and recommendations for further reading on each chapter, together with a brief review of each text, book chapter, or journal article cited.

Chapter 1

IPM Codes of Professional Conduct

The Institute of Personnel Management continues to emphasize and enforce minimum standards of professional practice in recruitment and selection among its members. The following represent essential reading for those responsible for all aspects of the selection process, including selection interviewing:

1   The IPM Recruitment Code, 1991
2   The IPM Code on Occupational Testing, 1990
3   The IPM Equal Opportunities Code, 1990
4   Age and Employment: An IPM Statement, 1991

All are available upon request from the IPM at

Institute of Personnel Management
IPM House
Camp Road
Wimbledon
LONDON SW19 4UX
Tel: 081 9469100

Chapter 2

Books on Selection Systems Generally

1   C. Lewis, *Employee Selection*, 2nd edn, (Hutchinson, London, 1992).
In the authors' view, probably the best dedicated introductory selection text aimed at students of HRM and Occupational Psychology. Affordable, readable, and preaches good professional practice in selection. Bridges the divide between academic research into selection and the day-to-day job demands of the recruiter with consumate ease. A valuable 'first purchase' for those new to the area of selection, and also a worthwhile refresher for those with so much experience as to have forgotten the academic principles of best practice.

2   P. Herriott, (ed) *Assessment and Selection in Organizations: Methods and practice for Recruitment and Appraisal*, (Wiley, Chichester, 1989).
The definitive handbook on selection and appraisal in Europe. Not to be carried around in one's jacket pocket for the occasional skim read, this text runs to forty four chapters and just over eight hundred pages! An essential reference text for specialists in selection, it also contains some intriguing case studies into the selection of manual workers, managers, professionals, computing staff, and military officers, among others.

3   M. Smith and I. T. Robertson (eds) *Advances in Selection and Assessment*, (Wiley, Chichester, 1989).
A thought-provoking mixture of twenty two chapters from academics and practitioners in Europe and the USA. Again, for the reader interested in a more sophisticated text aimed primarily at personnel psychology researchers and advanced practitioners in industry.

4   J. Arnold, I. T. Robertson and C. L. Cooper, *Work Psychology: Understanding Human Behaviour in the Workplace (Pitman, London, 1981)*.
A general textbook for the undergraduate and postgraduate student of work/organization psychology. Two excellent and concise chapters on the systems perspective of selection procedures. If you wish to gain a wider understanding of work psychology as a discipline, together with an introduction to the systems approach to selection, it is worth its very reasonable price tag designed to fit the student budget (loan).

5   M. Cook, *Personnel Selection and Productivity*, (Wiley, Chichester, 1988).
Makes a useful, if at times technical, addition to the company library of books on selection held in a typical HRM department. Covers aspects of the financial payback, or 'utility', of selection procedures in some detail.

6   P. Plumbley, *Recruitment and Selection*, (IPM Books, London, 1985).
An easy-to-read introductory text on how to establish basic procedures for recruitment and selection. Most valuable to those completely new to this area of personnel department activity.

Books on Job Analysis

1   M. Pearn and R. Kandola, *Job Analysis: A Practical Guide for Managers*, (IPM Books, London, 1988).
Does exactly as its title suggests – provides a practical guide into the methods and processes of job analysis. To be recommended as the first follow-up point of reference for those having read this book and needing a more detailed description of job analysis techniques than we were able to include here.

2   J. Algera and M. Greuter, *Job analysis for personnel selection*, (1989).
Laudable for its depth of coverage, this chapter was published in Mike Smith and Ivan Robertson's *Advances in Selection and Assessment* (1989), reviewed in the previous section. Deals with all aspects of job analysis – performance modelling, critical incident technique, work sampling, and other recent developments in the field. A striking example of one chapter from academics which should be influencing practice in industry – read it and you will gain an up-to-data knowledge of job analysis methodology.

Books on Psychometric Testing

1   J. Toplis V. Dulewitz and C. Fletcher, *Psychological Testing: A Practical guide for Employers*, (IPM Books, London, 1987).
Another in the IPM's valuable series of 'Practical Guides', this time offered up by three respected occupational psychologists, John Toplis, Vic Dulewitz, and Clive Fletcher. Again, in our view an ideal 'first point of call' for the reader wishing to delve into this subject in more detail.

2   J. Rust and S. Golombok, *Modern Psychometricians: The Science of Psychological Assessment*, (IPM Books, London, 1989).
More complex and comprehensive than the Toplis et al. text, this book constitutes the next level of difficulty for those interested in the technicalities of psychometrics. If you are thinking of buying-in psychological tests for your organization, read this book and you will be able to at least hold your own against the salespersons sent by test suppliers and publishers.

3 A. Annastasi, *Psychological Testing*, (Macmillan, New York, 1988).
Definitive and comprehensive coverage of the technicalities of psychological testing. A standard reference text in its area, Anne Annastasi shows all the signs of a master at work in her preferred field of specialism. Depth of coverage is the order of the day and so this book is only for those really wanting to gain a thorough and technical knowledge of test development and usage.

Chapter 3

Research Reviews

Regular reviews of the now voluminous number of interview research studies have been published in the academic psychology journals. Spanning some eighty years of research, these reviews make interesting reading for the dedicated bibliophile:

1 N. R. Anderson, 'Eight decades of employment interview research: A retrospective metareview and prospective commentary', *The European Work and Organizational Psychologist*, 2 (1992), 1–32.
2 M. M. Harris, 'Reconsidering the employment interview: A review of recent literature and suggestions for future research', *Personnel Psychology*, 42 (1989), 691–726.
3 R. D. Arvey and J. E. Campion, 'The employment interview: A summary and review of recent research', *Personnel Psychology*, 35 (1982) 281–322.
4 R. D. Arvey, 'Unfair discrimination in the employment interview: Legal and psychological aspects', *Psychological Bulletin*, 86 (1979), 736–765.
5 N. Schmitt, 'Social and situational determinants of interview decisions: Implications for the employment interview', *Personnel Psychology*, 29 (1976), 79–101.
6 O. P. Wright, 'Summary of research on the selection interview since 1964', *Personnel Psychology*, 22 (1969) 391–413.
7 L. Ulrich, and D. Trumbo, 'The selection interview since 1949', *Psychological Bulletin*, 63 (1965), 100–116.
8 E. C. Mayfield, 'The selection interview – A re-evaluation of published research', *Personnel Psychology*, 17 (1964), 239–260.
9 R. Wagner, 'The employment interview: A critical summary', *Personnel Psychology*, 2 (1949), 17–46.

Textbooks

Two seminal textbooks have been published in recent years which provide an in-depth coverage of interview practice based upon sound research principles:

R. L. Dipboye, *Selection Interviews: Process Perspectives*, (South-Western Publishing Co., Cincinnati, 1992).
R. W. Eder and G. R. Ferris (eds), *The Employment Interview: Theory, Research and Practice*, (Sage, London, 1989).

On the understanding that the reader has actually bought this book first, the authors recommend these two texts without reservation!

Chapter 4

1   T. Janz, L. Hellervik and D. C. Gilmore, *Behavior Description Interviewing*, (Allyn and Bacon Inc., Boston, 1986).
A detailed account of how to set up and conduct Patterned Behaviour Description Interviews. For the reader committed to establishing a highly structured assessment-phase interview, this book should prove a valuable reference source.

2.   P. Herriot, 'The selection interview' in *Psychology at Work*, ed. P. Warr (Penguin, Harmondsworth, 1987).
A thought-provoking chapter on interview functions and purposes also to be regarded as an essential follow-up for the interested reader. Specific social psychological theories (attribution theory, social exchange theory, among others) are evoked to account for errors in interviewer judgements. More theoretical in orientation, but one of the most innovative chapters on interviews to have appeared for years.

Chapters 5 and 6

We combine these chapters in terms of recommended further reading as both focus upon the essential skills of conducting successful selection interviews. Several sources for further reading can be recommended but only one to the knowledge of the authors explicitly adopts a cognitive-social skills approach to interviews as taken in this book. This is:

R. Millar, V. Crute and O. Hargie, *Professional Interviewing*, (Routledge, London, 1992).

A myriad of texts are to be found in libraries and on booksellers' shelves of the 'how to interview' ilk. Some useful, some restating the well-trodden paths in this area, and some downright misleading or patronizing. A selection which provides valuable follow-up coverage would include:

1 G. M. Breakwell, *Interviewing: Problems in Practice*, (BPS Books/ Routledge, London, 1990).
2 J. Courtis *Interviews: Skills and Strategy*, (IPM Books, London, 1988).
3 J. Fletcher *Effective Interviewing*; (Kogan Page, London, 1988).
4 M. Higham, *The ABC of Interviewing*, (IPM Books, London, 1979).
5 C. Roberts, *The Interview Game and How It's Played*, (BBC Publications, London, 1985).
6 C. Shouksmith, *Assessment Through Interviewing*, (Perganon Press, Oxford, 1978).

From the point of view of the candidate, fewer texts have been published on how to become a good interviewee. The most comprehensive and sensible is undoubtedly:

C. Fletcher, *Facing the Interview*, (Unwin Paperbacks, London, 1981).

Chapter 7

1 A. Rodger, 'The Seven Point Plan', *National Institute for Industrial Psychology*, Paper No 1.
2 J. Munro Fraser, *Employment Interviewing*, (MacDonald and Evans, London, 1978).

These texts provide details of the two most popular candidate assessment typologies Both are easy-to-read introductions on how to establish standardized criteria for selection interviewing (To be read in conjunction with the criticisms of standardized assessment typologies put forward in chapter 7.)

Chapter 8

Undoubtedly the first 'port of call' for follow-up reading concerning equal opportunities and unfair discrimination is the range of codes of practice currently in publication. These are issued by the British Psychological Society, the Commission for Racial Equality, and the Institute of Personnel Management. All of the following we would regard as essential reading for the recruiter:

1 British Psychological Society (1980)
   Discriminating Fairly: A Guide to Fair Selection
   The Runnymead Trust and The British Psychological Society
2 Commission for Racial Equality (1984)
   Code of Practice

The Elimination of Race Discrimination in Employment
HMSO, London
3   Equal Opportunities Commission (1985)
Code of Practice on Sex Discrimination
HMSO, London
4   Institute of Personnel Management
The IPM Equal Opportunities Code
IPM, London

In addition, those needing a more detailed coverage of the legislative provisions should consider consulting the major handbooks in this area. These are: Bowers (1990), Lewis (1990), Selwyn (1988), and Younson (1987). References to these are given at the end of chapter 8.

Chapter 9

The most extensive text for practitioners, which also includes practice exercises and case studies, is:

P. Hackett, *Interview Skills Training 3rd ed*, (IPM Books, London, 1990).

Author Index

Subject Index